D0872222

Moving Archives

The Experiences of Eleven Archivists

Edited by John Newman and
Walter Jones

The Scarecrow Press, Inc.
Lanham, Maryland, and Oxford
2002

SCARECROW PRESS, INC.

Published in the United States of America
by Scarecrow Press, Inc.
A Member of the Rowman & Littlefield Publishing Group
4720 Boston Way, Lanham, Maryland 20706
www.scarecrowpress.com

PO Box 317
Oxford
OX2 9RU, UK

British Library Cataloguing in Publication Information Available

Library of Congress Cataloging-in-Publication Data

Moving archives : the experiences of eleven archivists / edited by John
  Newman and Walter Jones.
        p. cm.
    Includes bibliographical references.
    ISBN 0-8108-4500-8 (alk. paper)
    1. Archival moving—United States—Case studies. I. Newman, John,
  1942- . II. Jones, Walter, 1944-

    CD3021.M68 2002
    027—dc21   2002010299

Contents

Acknowledgments

Editors John Newman and Walter Jones are grateful to a number of professional colleagues for their assistance and support in completing this book. First among these people is Dale Askey, librarian at the University of Utah, who gave invaluable advice on formatting the book's various sections. Others, whose technical assistance proved to be highly important at the University of Utah, are librarian Kenning Arlitsch and computer specialists Julia Brown and Jeremy Sharpe. At Colorado State University's Archives, Pat Vandeventer read and commented upon the entire text. The editors are grateful to the chapter authors who have agreed unanimously to donate all royalties to The Society of American Archivists' Donald Peterson Student Scholarship Fund.

Preface

Walter Jones and I formed the idea for this book in conversations that began in the late 1990s. We had each moved large collections and found little written anywhere to guide us. Later, we discovered that this experience was shared by other archivists. Our goal here is to provide an initial piece of professional literature in what we hope will become a growing body of modern information about moving archives.

To measure interest in the subject and to expand our knowledge, Professor Jones and I led a session on moving archives at the joint meeting of the Northwest Archivists, the Conference of Intermountain Archivists, the Society of Rocky Mountain Archivists and the Northwest Oral History Association on May 26, 2001. The session was well attended and the papers were interesting. Several of the authors whose chapters follow were recruited there.

As we developed the idea, we identified more contributors and incorporated their views. It says something about the nature of the members of our profession, at least of those who are tasked to manage large moves, that everyone agreed we should emphasize practical matters and avoid much attempt to articulate theory. Every archive and every move are different, and our intent is that anyone who seeks guidance from this work will find at least one account here that is helpful for the situation he or she faces.

Common approaches and practices emerge from these pages because the contributors' experiences have followed similar paths. My impression is that most people know little about our work. If they think of us at all, they may imagine that we spend our days in the quiet and meticulous examination of ancient documents. In fact, many archivists I know often work in relative ignorance and haste, handling new collections and circumstances with little preparation and too few staff, and demonstrate qualities of energy, expediency and imagination.

Archivists learn not to be intimidated by tons, or tens of tons, of paper, however precious. Experience has taught us, too, that plans may be changed abruptly and dramatically as collections reveal themselves to us, conditions alter, or the minds of administrators change. We are accustomed to accepting responsibility for valuable records in physical and administrative environments that are often precarious. In short, routine archival work is good preparation for moving large collections and entire repositories.

In this book, each writer speaks in his or her own voice and describes a unique situation. Fortunately, alphabetical order places Lisa Backman's chapter first. Hers is the most general treatment, drawing lessons from her extensive experience. Indeed, she points a way that might be taken by any more theoretical book on this subject. She also anticipates many of the general lessons in the chapters that follow.

In describing the move at the Oklahoma Department of Libraries, Gary Harrington conveys just how complex both timing and physical aspects of a large move can become. He also makes a case for detailed planning and careful coordination with professional movers and, indeed, with all other persons involved. He points out, as well, how phase one of his move helped prepare for phase two.

Walter Jones' experience at the University of Utah also involved two moves; the staff learned from the first how better to manage the second. As with the Oklahoma move, the faculty and staff at the University of Utah dealt with very complex issues of timing. They managed, as well, to address the service concerns of several groups, including administrators, faculty and patrons. An additional complication at Utah was the requirement to move rare books as well as archives and manuscripts.

Monte Kniffen brings the perspective and style of a traditionally trained scholar to his description of the project by an earlier archivist to combine two archives and libraries of the Redemptorists into a third facility in Denver. He points out, especially, the problems associated with long-distance moves, including a matter of damage claims. Like many other archives, the Redemptorists' move was associated with a renovation, and that added its own set of "unanticipated events."

Very detailed planning and preparation characterized Joanne Mattern's move of the Delaware Public Archives. Her ability to craft clear explanations of complicated matters probably had something to do with her success in a move that was both very complex and documented in detail. She conveys a lively sense of the determination that must have helped her manage relationships with commercial movers. Her extensive summary of lessons learned reinforces the very similar views expressed by Lisa Backman.

When I relocated the Colorado State University Archives, I thought no archivist ever had moved so much, so far, so well. I see now, that compared to the others here, mine was a small, simple effort. Like everyone, we planned in detail, but, in fact, we had less to plan and less to do. That everything went so well is due in large part to the karate black belt "volunteers" who were drafted to assist.

What Patrick Quinn faced in 1966 moving archives at the State Historical Society of Wisconsin will resonate with those old enough to remember Kardex files and typewriters. Little enough had changed by 1994 that he could still draw useful lessons for his move of the Northwestern University Archives. Planning and preparation were still central, and flexibility was still required. His third "bonus" move of Law School and Medical School records in 1999 confirmed what he had already learned. Boxes were no lighter, but successful experience brought confidence. Like others, Mr. Quinn offers a good summary of lessons learned.

Russell C. Taylor introduces the chilling term "million" into his description of the glass plates that were part of the huge move at Brigham Young University. His was a massive undertaking, involving numerous locations and a serious concern for physical security. He emphasizes the importance of staff supervision of everything and the value of learning from the experience of others. A realist, Mr. Taylor describes some of the problems that are still being solved.

At the University of Colorado, Cassandra Volpe describes how she is planning a move that will take place later this year. By focusing just on planning, Ms. Volpe brings proper emphasis to the point made by everyone that planning is absolutely essential. She, too, confronts complex and ever-changing issues with facilities. This careful preparation will help her achieve success, despite the surprises that she will almost certainly encounter.

Albin Wagner emerges from a scholarly tradition similar to Monte Kniffen. He puts his institution and his move in proper historical context and writes with the assured tone of someone who knows exactly what he is doing—even in the third person. A competent disaster plan for the Rhode Island State Records Center provided the basis for his rapid and flexible response to a fire that revealed asbestos problems. Mr. Wagner successfully managed what must be the most dramatic situation represented in this book.

At the Oregon Historical Society, Todd Welch had only six months to locate and move to a new facility. Pressure of time and the inherent complexity of collections led to the employment of both consultants and professional movers. Mr. Welch conveys a textbook account of techniques to integrate such outsiders with professional staff as well as how to impose both intellectual and operational control on a situation with an amazing number of variables.

Everyone here has done so well in their moves. Each archivist confronted complexity and uncertainty with a good plan and a flexible attitude. Each learned as he or she went along, dealt with surprises that could not have been anticipated and remained composed. In the end, the public, the agencies and the patrons served by these archivists were served well.

Perhaps it is not too much to say that in preserving the integrity of their collections while moving them, these archivists have also served posterity well.

John Newman
Colorado State University Archives

The Cable Center

Lisa Backman

In the years that I have been in Denver working in archives and with manuscripts, I have managed to move a part or an entire collection nearly every other year. I have recently completed my third move in one and one-half years at The Cable Center. This brings the number of moves that I have participated in to eleven. The collections that have been moved have ranged from a small portion going from one floor to another, which was done on book carts, to working with professional movers transferring over twelve thousand feet of manuscripts from a warehouse to permanent shelving. (Oops, in our business, no housing is ever permanent.)

The circumstances surrounding the moves have varied widely. When I was involved with a large move, the movers were chosen by bid with very little input from those who were in charge of the material. When I was involved in a small move, I not only personally knew the facility people that were helping but also donned my gloves and did my share. So the following is some advice that I hope will prove useful and make your move a little smoother.

The Planning Stages

From the very beginning, everyone that will be involved with your move should be included. This means that all must attend any meetings where the upcoming move is discussed—planning a move is not the time for hierarchies, meaning supervisors and managers attend some meetings and the rest of the employees attend others. These meetings might involve discussing the type of shelving, the schematics of rooms, the organization on the shelves, staff responsibilities, and any number of subjects. Everyone brings invaluable experience with them. Admittedly, not everyone needs to be in on the final decisions regarding every aspect such as budget, but it is still very important to have the input of the people responsible for the material and for the move. There are many "experts" (library designers, administrators, salespeople) who will be giving their advice, but when it comes time to actually implement the move and put the material up on the shelves, it is the staff that works with the material that knows it best. Ultimately, everyone must be on the same page. Communication is the key to a successful move.

All information and decisions that are made in the planning stages need to be consistent and given to everyone. Make sure all the decisions are in writing. For example, when we were moving manuscript collections that were stored in record storage boxes, the fact that they needed to be kept in order was discussed in two meetings but never put in writing. On the day of the move, the moving supervisor never heard those instructions and thought the boxes could go anywhere on the shelves. If those instructions had been in writing, there would have been no surprises for the movers. They would have fully understood the situation. It does not hurt to plot, plan, and plot again. To quote various carpenters "measure twice, cut once." I cannot reiterate too many times; make sure everyone knows the final decisions and all information regarding the move is made available to everyone.

Move Coordinator

A staff coordinator must be appointed. This person needs to know every minute detail such as: the timeline, who the contact for the movers is, what staff member has been assigned to what responsibility and he/she must be willing to follow-up on those assignments to make sure everyone has and does their job. This person needs to be given the responsibility to and have the ability to make decisions. They also need to know what is moving where and how. In some cases, a large institution will need more than one coordinator, but if all decisions are in writing then any coordinator can cover for the others. The coordinator is the person the movers will be talking directly to. It is a position that carries a lot of responsibility and can be very detailed oriented.

Working with Outside Moving Companies

First and foremost, interview movers. Many of us have to put bids out because we work for government agencies or we want the most economical company, but a mover with absolutely no experience with the type of material they will be handling is not cost effective. Try to get a mover who has experience with libraries or archives. If that is not possible, make sure that the mover listens, asks questions, takes notes on what is expected, and asks to see the material. After a company has been contracted, talk to your movers. Do they understand the type of material that you are moving? Is it boxes of books or boxes of fragile museum collectibles? Do they understand the system that you have devised for moving?

Movers all have their own instructions on how to move. Where possible make sure you pack your material according to their standards. It will save you time following the movers instructions rather than having to unpack. For example, one moving company may feel it is okay to leave a file cabinet full, while another company may want you to empty out the top two drawers for balance. The mover may have suggestions for moving odd items that you had not thought of, such as wardrobe boxes for rolled architectural drawings. Getting the instructions ahead of time also allows you to discuss with the movers types of materials that may not be included in their lists. Since we also have instructions for the movers, keep them as simple as possible. It is not unusual for an extended move to have different crews from day to day. If possible, mark your material in straightforward numerical system. Color coding in some instances may be useful. Do not expect the movers to understand or learn your series systems. They quite honestly are not getting paid to learn series or subseries. Again, keep things simple but make sure that the movers know what to expect such as what is fragile material and what your expectations are and instructions are.

Know the moving supervisor. Not just the contact person at the moving company, but the crew supervisor. It is not always the friendliest and most outgoing person who makes a point of introducing himself. Seek the crew supervisor out. Do this every day of your move because, once again, it may not be the same person from day to day. The supervisor is the person you will be discussing all moving matters with. Make a friend. As an aside, occasionally, you will come across people on the moving team who decide they know exactly what is going on, decide they can do it better and begin to give everyone instructions. Unless this has gone through the supervisor and you, do not let this happen. The instructions can run counter to the plan already in place. If part of the moving team comes up with a good idea, make sure you and the supervisor have okayed it. Stay on top of the move!

Before your move, walk through all areas with the moving supervisor to locate all material and possible moving routes. The height and width of doors and elevators are all very important. If an elevator is involved with the move, find out who has the key and how to stop the elevator for loading and unloading. Also, think about parking for the vans. We had a situation where the movers almost brought a van that was too large for the parking lot and another situation where the van was too tall for an overhang. If necessary, make sure you have cones to block off the parking spaces. It is not fun to have to locate the owner of a car that is parked where the moving van needs to pull up to.

Finally, before you begin your move know how your mover bills. Is it by job or is it an hourly rate? Know what constitutes a change order. If a change is necessary as you are moving your material, discuss it with the move supervisor and how it can be handled. Changes and problems do arise in the middle of a move, but remember it is your money and you do not want any surprises on the final bill.

More Practical Matters

The Material

We know our material. We know how to retrieve it. We know how to handle it. Never assume that those who will be moving the material do. It is all new to them. So here are a few very simple suggestions. First, label everything clearly. Secondly, if the material is going into very specific locations, keep the location guide very clear and simple. For example, as I mentioned before, number your items consecutively. Do not try to explain that this collection has four boxes and that one has six. Just start at the beginning with the number one and keep going until you get to the end. If the material is going to different sections within one room, then color-coding with dots or different inks will be fine, but again, number consecutively. In addition to your own numbering, movers will usually supply you with different colored labels. These are used to identify the different rooms or areas where material is going to. The coordinator should make sure that workers have enough labels for the material that they are responsible for.

We all want our collections to look very neat and organized on the shelf but do not worry about the moving labels. If you put them on the boxes where the movers suggest, they usually will not interfere with the labels that are already identifying the boxes. Also, if you remove the moving labels as soon as possible, there is less likelihood that they will be permanently stuck to your boxes.

Shelving

Measure, measure, measure. Make sure the material is going to fit on the shelving that you are moving onto. This is not always as straightforward as it may seem. Frequently, many of us have done moves where the material goes first and then the shelving. If you are moving everything exactly as it was before, you may not have any problems, but if different material is going up on the shelves be prepared to make some snap decisions. The majority of your boxes will fit, but there will definitely be items that will not.

Also, the actual shelving units may not fit where you think they will. Measure not only the actual shelves but measure the height and width. We have had temporary panics where we discovered that the old shelving that we were moving into a new location would not only not fit through the doors but was also too tall for the room. Some quick action and we were able to move other shelving into the room. In our case, we were lucky.

Labeling

I already mentioned labeling the boxes. That seems like common sense. Do not forget while you are at it to label the aisles and if possible label the shelves. Make a map of the room where your material is being moved to and label that map to coincide with all your other locations. Make sure that all of this information is handy to the movers and to all the coordinators and then make extra copies. I have had to loan my location guide only to never get it back and then need it for an additional move a short while later. It's not a waste of paper. Not having the location guides convenient and in multiple copies can cause a lot of frustration.

Staffing

There must be someone with the movers at all times. Why should you have staff member available at all times? To answer questions and solve problems that arise and need to be resolved immediately. Questions such as directions to go in a building or someone to hold the elevator door when the key does not work are all simple matters that can be handled quickly with a staff member available. When problems occur, if a staff member is readily available, the movers do not have to wait around while searching for someone to solve that problem. For example, it is surprising how many boxes miss being labeled or somehow get separated from the group they are supposed to be with; the staff member can identify that material right away. Also, the staff member is able to keep an eye on everything to make sure nothing gets left behind. It is very important to do a final walk through after the move. Every moving company will require that you do a final walk through with the moving supervisor, but before the doors of the moving van are closed, do your own walk around. Items do inadvertently get missed. Most importantly, it is a matter of security having a staff member with the movers at all times. No one likes to admit that items can go missing, but items can and do go missing.

One More Suggestion

After the movers have left and everything is on the shelf, do not hold off on your shelf reading. Time goes by very quickly and it is not too soon before a request from a researcher comes in and you then discover you can not locate an item that was recently shifted. Shelf read immediately. Build this task right into your moving plan. It is much easier to see what may have been misshelfed while it is fresh in your mind than to pick up the task again, especially after life gets back to normal. No one likes the surprise of finding a box completely separated from its location by an entire room, or, if you have colored coded, you then discover a blue dot in the middle of the red dots.

The Wrap Up

There are several essential things to remember in order to conduct a successful move. First, plan well. Then communicate with everyone involved, both in writing and verbally. In addition, know your movers and know their needs to make the move go smoothly.

My Final Advice

Common sense? Forget it. Assume anything? Never. We all know what assume means. Did you plan for every problem that could possibly occur? Probably not. Did something you never thought could occur happen? Yes, it probably did. While most of the suggestions are for larger moves, I hope the suggestions helped ease the way a little bit for both small and large moves. Just remember—everything will get moved and it really does work out in the end.

Oklahoma Department of Libraries

Gary Harrington

The Oklahoma State Archives and Records Management Divisions are housed in two distinct locations. The State Archives maintains over 27,000 cubic feet of permanent state agency records and is located on the third floor of the Allen Wright Memorial Library building in Oklahoma City. The State Records Center, 21st Street, maintains over 40,000 cubic feet of impermanent records from state agencies and is located two blocks north of the main library. It has been occupied since 1975 with a major renovation occurring in 1982. In the past we have also leased another facility, 13th Street, about one and a half miles from the records center.

The need for additional space and an improved storage and office environment resulted in the decision to survey available buildings to lease for an extended period of time and one that would meet our expansion requirements. After inspecting several sites, some of which proved to be beyond our budget and others not suitable by location, the owner of one such site contacted our agency through the Department of Central Services, the state's leasing agent. The facility was being used as a tire recapping service and was not considered suitable for the storage of records.

The owner and operator of the facility of the tire recapping service were very mindful of our requirements. A portion of the building is already leased by two other Oklahoma state agencies. We expressed our concerns about the space available and current housekeeping. The owner was building another facility for his recapping service and was moving out in early 2000. After his move he would convert the warehouse to meet our needs: renovation, cleaning, and painting. To accommodate our space requirement, the owner also agreed to build an additional, 50' x 170', structure onto the west side of the original warehouse. This addition would contain new office space of 50' x 65' which would allow for general offices and space for our micrographics laboratory.

The owner had promised a move-in date to the original warehouse by the early spring of 2000. Due to other construction commitments, Oklahoma weather, city, county, and state inspection requirements we did not take formal occupancy of the warehouse until July 2000.

Phase One: Preparation and Planning

Prior to the movement of records and shelving from the 13th Street facility, our first leased building, administrative and support staff formulated a plan of action. We knew that we were going to move but did not have a definite move-in date since owner deadlines continued to change. The 13th Street facility contained over 10,730 boxes and three map cabinets (flat files) of state agency records. There was also compact and other high-density shelving to be broken down, transported, and then reassembled.

Support staff had also visited and inspected the Hill Street warehouse for further shelving needs. We were in constant communication with the owner and his contractor concerning areas that would require maintenance before our possession and move in.

The first step was to calculate the amount and location of high-density shelving sections needed to finish filling the original Hill Street warehouse. Secondly, we had no further use for the compact shelving and were looking for a buyer.

The plan of action included removing boxes from the compact shelving, having a buyer remove the compact shelving, contacting a mover, and ordering new ten-foot, high-density shelving sections.

As with most state governments, to procure services that are above a financial limit, one must send requirements out for bid. Within Oklahoma this is accomplished through the Department of Central Services. Usually the low bidder gets the job. Naturally part of this process is writing the specifications for the job to be performed. A person must be specific but flexible because dates and supplies change.

For our needs we required a bid for a mover and another for the additional shelving sections. The coordination for the time of delivery and the physical move were being planned for the last days of July 2000.

Prior to the movement of shelving and records from 13th Street, the Hill Street facility had to be prepared. The current and ordered shelving sections had to be preassigned a position. A structural floor plan was designed and the shelving sizes and amount of sections were accounted for. After the warehouse was renovated according to our needs, and with the owner's approval, division staff measured and chalked specific shelving section locations allowing four feet of aisle space as well as for future growth. Of course, these were estimates since plans do sometimes vary with reality.

The Move

We finally found a buyer for the compact shelving. Knowing that we needed to remove these shelves as soon as possible, the three-person division staff had emptied it in earlier weeks. Most of the boxed records were placed on pallets and shrink-wrapped. Other records were transferred to other shelves at our 21st Street facility. The removal of the shelving was accomplished one week before the scheduled move of the other shelved records.

The scheduled receipt of the new high-density shelf sections was delayed by one week due to the manufacturer. The companies that ordered and assembled the new shelving sections were also committed to break down and reassemble shelf sections already owned. Rather than start assembling the new shelf sections in its predetermined location, we had to start by breaking down the shelf sections at the 13th Street building.

We had hoped that the movers would be removing and placing boxes on pallets at 13th Street while the shelvers were assembling shelves at Hill Street. With this change we now had movers and shelving assemblers at 13th Street.

The movers used three semi-trailers and two forklifts, one each at 13th Street and Hill Street. Eleven men were used to remove boxes from the shelves, shrink-wrap, and forklift to a truck, and then travel to Hill Street for unloading. The pallets were stored in a vacant area of the Hill Street warehouse until the shelf sections were reassembled. The movers had allotted three days for the move.

When a section of shelves was emptied, it was disassembled and loaded to trucks. After all records were moved to Hill Street, the movers left and were rescheduled to return after the shelf sections had been reassembled and were ready for reshelving. At this time the new order of shelf sections was received. It would take five days for the shelf sections to be reassembled.

All shelf sections and storage records boxes (10,730 cubic feet) were moved July 17-28, 2000. The new high-density shelves that had arrived were also assembled at this time.

Three members of our office staff were delegated the tasks of site observers and coordinators. Their duties were to make sure that records were loaded onto pallets by section. Each section held thirty-five boxes, therefore one pallet contained only thirty-five boxes. A staff member labeled each pallet with the original location before it was wrapped for shipment.

The phase one operation was completed during the first week of August. The movers returned, and pallets were moved to specific locations for the boxes to be shelved. New locations were noted on an inventory for later computer input and update.

Building Addition Preparation

Phase one of our move proved to be a learning experience in preparation for the next move that would not only involve the movement of records but the relocation of three offices from the 21st Street facility to Hill Street. The second move would include office furniture, electronic equipment, micrographics equipment (cameras, and processing equipment), and the relocation of nine staff members.

The Hill Street facility, as earlier noted, not only involved the renovation of the warehouse but a 50' x 170' addition. The addition would have 50' x 65' dedicated for new office space. A customer reference area, micrographics laboratory and office, a conference room, a break room, and two additional offices for records management and supervision were planned. The blueprints had been developed and approved by the owner and our supervision prior to start. The Department of Central Services also had to approve the plans based upon space allocation to each staff member.

The building addition was hoped to begin in the spring of 2000. However, due to a wet spring and contractor commitments, work on the addition did not begin until August with the pouring of the concrete slab. Work slowly began on the walls and roof. These had to be completed before the fall and winter season arrived. The office wall studding was set in place during November while the roof was being completed. The heating, ventilation, and air conditioning (HVAC) systems for the offices were placed as well as a hot water source for the break room and restrooms.

Before walls were put in place, four of our agency staff from Management Information Systems (MIS) and the Web Development Office ran computer and telephone cable. This eliminated most hanging cables to individual staff desks and also saved the agency money.

Final office preparations were being done during December.

A problem did arise during construction concerning our micrographics laboratory. During the pouring of the slab and future building it was noted that no drainage, water supply, and sink had been planned for based on the blueprints for our processing room. This had been addressed earlier and was remedied during the office construction.

In January 2001, after all city, county, and state inspections were performed, we were ready to occupy the new office and warehouse areas.

Phase Two: Preparation and Planning

Time was short for the upcoming move. Our division staff had begun to pack non-essential office records and various pieces of equipment in advance. An inventory of all that was to be moved was developed and submitted for bid in early January. The bid was awarded to the same movers from phase one. The movers were to begin on January 22nd and finish by January 26th.

Since the Records Management Division serves state government and the public it was determined that we would close our offices on January 22nd and reopen on February 5th. Advance notification was sent to all state agencies and posted for our in-person customers.

Computers and equipment at the 21st Street facility were disconnected and moved to Hill Street by our MIS division one week prior to the movers scheduled moving date.

The plan of action included removing boxes from 21st Street facility, placing these boxes on pallets and hauling them to Hill Street, removing all necessary office furniture and equipment and hauling it to Hill Street, and relocating office furniture and equipment.

With such a narrow window of opportunity, all records center staff would be involved in the move and were responsible for individual office set up. Three staff members and one supervisor were responsible for records removal from existing shelves and their movement to Hill Street. Division staff would be responsible for the unloading of pallets to shelving once the move was complete.

Records to be moved from the 21st Street facility were located on two floors with only one slow and small elevator to move approximately eight thousand boxes of records. The problem was overcome with some ingenuity by the creation of a temporary chute. The second floor of the 21st Street building is an open mezzanine with rails. The movers removed a section of the railing and created a temporary box chute. It was labor intensive but effective.

The Move

The movers arrived on January 22nd to perform a preliminary evaluation of the 21st Street building. They were shown the records and office furniture and equipment to be moved which were located in all areas of the building. At this point they reviewed the use of the elevator and decided to manufacture a temporary box chute. The crew returned on January 23rd to get their equipment in place. Once again they used three semi-trailers and two forklifts, one at each location.

Only two state agency records were going to be moved. The records are maintained by calendar year but may be divided based upon space available at the time of accessioning. To make sure that the records were maintained and packed in order, the movers were requested to follow our direction. To this end the records were removed by year and placed on pallets for transfer.

Staff members monitored the movement closely since several teams of movers operated in different areas of the warehouse. Checklists, previously developed, were used to verify that the appropriate shelf sections had been cleared of records.

After records had been placed on pallets and loaded into a truck, the truck went to Hill Street where a staff member coordinated the unloading and temporary storage of the pallet in the new-addition warehouse. Once all of the records were removed from 21st Street and hauled to Hill Street, they would eventually be placed on specific shelf sections by our staff.

The initial phase of this move, the warehouse records, was accomplished in two and one-half days. The office furniture and equipment was completed within the day and involved all division staff. Once everything was on the truck, the staff then moved to Hill Street for furniture placement within their individual offices.

The set up and connections of computer and micrographics equipment would follow the next week.

Follow Up

After the move of records, furniture, and equipment the following week staff was delegated the task of getting set up and organized for our reopening on February 5th. A number of staff had to move loaded pallets to areas where the records were to be reshelved. Eight thousand boxes had to be shelved in order, inventoried, and location-listed by February

2nd. Over the next five days, as many as five staff members were involved in the placement of the boxes.

The customer-office area was organized and ready for business on February 5th. The micrographics laboratory was up and ready except for some minor alterations involving hot water and electrical circuitry. These problems would be resolved in the next few months.

As an auxiliary site, the computer link to the main library required that we purchase a T-1 line and maintain an off-site server for our specific use. Coordination between our MIS division, the telephone company, and another state agency eventually brought our system to standards within two months.

Successes

There were a number of successful events that occurred during both phases of these planned movements.

The foremost and critical aspect was to be involved with the owner and operator of a warehouse that will accept your storage requirements within a reasonable time and cost. Not only was the owner able to renovate an existing warehouse but he also responded to our need for additional warehouse and new office space. He had an involved contractor and various subcontractors who worked with our staff and supervision. They met most of our requirements. Deadlines were set by the owner, but due to other commitments by the contractors and the Oklahoma weather, they were usually set back. Patience and a flexible time-line should always be considered.

Be flexible. Do not expect deadlines to be met. Concerning the ordering and receipt of new shelf sections, we learned that no matter what your time line, unexpected changes will occur. We set time and event lines for efficiency, but most frequently a multitude of problems arise. Be prepared to have an alternative plan. In the case of the ordered shelf sections, the manufacturer could not meet the delivery date. Therefore, the movers and shelving companies personnel had to work in close quarters. The movers had to stop and return several days later to reshelf boxes at Hill Street.

Have a plan. It should contain the goal. How to obtain that goal will depend on specific needs. What needs are critical to one's operation and which are important? With the Phase I move, our need was based on a lease deadline at 13th Street. We had to be moved by the end of August 2000. We acquired the Hill Street warehouse on July 10, 2000. Therefore, we had a small window for movement. But by anticipating the acquisition of Hill Street, we had already planned for the order of new shelf sections, the breakdown and reinstallation of current shelf sections, and the movement of boxes at least a month in advance. We had to take into account the amount of time involved in the current bid requirements, which at times delays an operation.

Data information about records in the State Records Center is housed within an Access software program specifically adapted for our needs. Their specific accession number, state agency name, and title of record are used to locate records. The records are then allocated a location based upon row and section. The phase one and two moves involved extensive amendments to our computer data. It was critical during the two moves to maintain the past location and reallocate the new location first by a visual inspection and then by updating our current system. It was necessary to always have staff on site at both locations to monitor these changes and to maintain the site's security.

The lessons learned from the phase one move helped during the phase two operation. Similar to phase one, phase two involved a move from one area to another but also included office relocation. Early in 2000, we knew that our offices would be moving. The only question was, "when?" Since the deadline kept changing, staff was instructed to plan the movement of necessary furniture and equipment. Non-essential records and equipment were boxed and ready to move. Each staff member had responsibilities and succeeded in an efficient and timely move. Staff cooperation and morale was high.

To parallel staff cooperation, the support of the agency administration is very necessary. Without their help a plan will either continue very slowly or fail. Cooperation and support from all levels certainly is positive and will see the project through to the end.

Failures

I do not believe that failures occurred during the movements. Admittedly, some deadlines were not met but we adapted. Perhaps a breakdown in communication did occur regarding our building needs for the addition; needs concerning micrographics electrical requirements, plumbing, and ventilation were overlooked in the blueprints.

New warehouse ventilation had not been addressed until the walls and roof were completed. These problems have since been resolved. Other problems will continue to come up but as long as we maintain an active communication link with the owner we hope to maintain an efficient and effective state agency operation.

Acknowledgments

I am indebted to the records management staff, including Bill Boone, Tina Calloway, Evans Elie, George Asbill, Rancy Thompson, Linda Colbert, Renee Nixon, and Diana Ledford. In addition, I would also like to thank the staff of the Oklahoma Department of Libraries for their support and cooperation. These people are Robert L. Clark, Director (retired); Susan McVey, Director; Vicki Sullivan; Barbara Riddle; Kristi Hawkins; Michael O'Hasson; Mike Adams; Larry Dobbs; Rich Owens; and Steve Beleu.

University of Utah

Walter Jones

In this chapter I will deal with two moves that the University of Utah's J. Willard Marriott Library's Special Collections Department made in the late 1990s. The first move took place in the spring of 1998, and the second move occurred in the spring and early summer of 1999. I will cover topics that include our planning, decisions, and experiences regarding each move.

By way of background, those divisions of Special Collections which became involved in the two moves are Manuscripts, Middle East, Multi-Media Archives, Rare Books with its Book Arts Studio facilities, and Western Americana which also manages Special Collections University of Utah published or printed archives materials such as dissertations, catalogues, and bulletins. At the time of the first move, these divisions with their collections, facilities and staffs were housed on the J. Willard Marriott Library's top or fifth floor where they occupied approximately 55 percent of the floor's 42,000 square feet of floor space. Regarding collections, Special Collections consists of a large variety of materials that include manuscripts, photographs, monographs, serials, newspapers, vertical and clipping files, maps, microfilm, architectural drawings, and a book press with its accompanying book-arts equipment.

In 1994, the University of Utah began a two-year-long construction program to add 200,000 square feet to the existing J. Willard Marriott Library. This construction program resulted in Special Collections' becoming the sole occupant of the entire fifth floor of the library, but before this occupation happened a series of events unfolded over a six-year period that required the department to conduct the two moves it made in the late 1990s.

Special Collections' sequence of events began in 1992 when the assistant director for the department gathered his staff to begin to plan for the eventual location of each of the department's divisions on the library's fifth floor once the construction project ended. This early planning was elementary, involving the study of floor space available and the possible location of the department's various divisions. Over the next five years, Special Collections' staff adopted an attitude of watch and wait, and no definite plan emerged regarding the exact location for any division.

Shortly after contractors completed the 200,000 square-foot addition to the Marriott Library in 1996, a new set of contractors started to "retrofit" the old portion of the library. This retrofit work included upgrading the library's fire-suppression system as well as removing the building's asbestos. The work began on the bottom floor of the Marriott Library and proceeded at a rate of one floor every six months which gave Special Collections nearly two years to plan and prepare for the work to be done on the fifth floor. Near the end of these two years the library removed all fifth-floor operations not connected to Special Collections. Approximately 45 percent of the floor became vacant, allowing contractors to retrofit these unoccupied areas.

During the three months that retrofit employees worked on the vacant portion of the fifth floor, Special Collections' assistant director and staff began to plan for its first of the two moves. It became immediately clear that this first move would be the more simple of the two. Each Special Collections division would move into a completely vacant area, and nothing would have to move off of the fifth floor. Also, since the move would be into temporary quarters, only the minimum amount of planning and coordination within and without the department would be required.

Special Collections' staff members met infrequently but often enough to make several key decisions regarding the first move. The first important decision related to the location of each collection. While this decision took the most time to complete and was the hardest of the initial decisions to make, everyone involved in the move cooperated to the extent that the decision-making process went smoothly. Harmony prevailed despite the fact that no one was happy with the amount of space allotted to his or her division.

A second key decision was to keep a reference desk open during the move so that patrons could receive some, albeit limited, assistance. Accordingly, Special Collections' staff decided to conduct a limited public relations campaign to notify potential visitors that reduced reference service would be available. The department's Multi-media Archives curator volunteered to send press releases to various agencies in the Salt Lake City area.

During the planning stage for the move, the Assistant Director for Special Collections informed the various division heads that the separate reference desks for Manuscripts, Rare Books and Western Americana would be combined into one location in the new area and that this combined reference desk would remain in operation after the final move. While this concept was not easy to implement, the division heads involved planned ways of integrating staffs for cross training and for desk schedules.

Another important decision was to use library-wide moving crews to move the majority of Western Americana and printed archives' collections. Since the building's existing moving crews had extensive experience in moving large collections of materials into the library's new addition, Western Americana's staff felt that the crews would handle Special Collections published materials adequately.

As the department's first move began and progressed, several problems arose. Immediately, Special Collections' patrons became unhappy with the idea of reduced service. Several visitors, not learning of the move, traveled considerable distances with the expectation that they could receive full reference service. The second problem to arise was Special Collections had so little time to move that all outside support providers had either to work too fast to do a thorough job or had to use easily available materials to satisfy the need for temporary support. Janitors, for instance, had no time to clean the department's floors properly while the carpenter shop could only provide unpleasant looking wire-mesh walls to seal off the restricted areas of the floor. The overall result of this rapidly completed work was the creation of a temporary area that had a prisonlike, dirty physical appearance. Over time, these conditions, combined with the cramped nature of the temporary work and storage spaces, produced an extremely unpleasant job environment.

The final major problem encountered during of the move was the mishandling of Western Americana's collections because the movers had not been trained to treat old, fragile, and rare materials properly. The crews that came to assist Western Americana worked fast but lacked the experience they needed to provide careful handling for the division's materials. This situation caused Western Americana's staff to rethink the idea of using outside crews to assist in the final move.

Overall, the first move was bumpy and problem ridden, yet it gave to the department's staff an excellent set of experiences from which to develop a strategy for the second move. Given a "lessons learned" frame of reference and recognizing that this next move would be more complicated, Special Collections' full-time employees started meeting every two weeks immediately after the first move to begin planning for the second move. While the assistant director for Special Collections was in charge of the meetings and gave these sessions his administrative requirements, goals and support, the responsibility of leading the meetings' discussions and creating a detailed plan transferred to the head of Western Americana, the author of this chapter.

One of the first topics of the meetings was the sequence of each division's move. Since the department would take over the entire fifth floor of the library, the divisions involved, Manuscripts, Middle East, Multi-media Archives, Rare Books, and Western Americana would have the opportunity to expand their collection, office and work areas. This meant, however, that some divisions would be in the way of others at the beginning of the move. While Manuscripts, Multi-media Archives, and Rare Books' Book Arts materials would move into completely vacant portions of the fifth floor, Middle East, Rare Books, and Western Americana would have to arrange their moves so that one move followed another. In their temporary locations, Western Americana's collections sat where Middle East would go, Middle East occupied much of the area that was to become Rare Books' area, and Rare Books' temporary shelving overlapped the area that Western Americana would ultimately take over. This complicated the planning but was finally resolved when Western Americana's staff agreed to move and compact all of that division's collections into the portion of its new floor space that was ready to receive materials. In doing this, Middle East could then occupy 100 percent of its new area and Rare Books could move completely into all of its permanent quarters.

As this assertive, cooperative type of planning progressed, the department's staff quickly seized the opportunity to request new archival shelving for Manuscripts and Multi-media Archives. In addition, the employees strongly suggested that the ugly wire-mesh walls be replaced with more secure and aesthetically pleasant glass walls as barriers to the restricted collections. Also, the staff insisted that all of the floor areas be cleaned properly this time before occupying any of them. The acquisition of new shelving, the installation of glass walls and the thorough cleaning of all Special Collections' areas required extensive coordinating with the library's facilities and building managers, with outside vendors, and with the University of Utah's fire marshal, carpenter shop and janitorial offices.

As Special Collections' employees planned the second move, various staff members compiled a laundry list of needs that became apparent during the first move. One of the most disappointing failures of the first move was that of attempting to provide reduced reference service. This activity failed because people continued to demand full service despite the disruptive nature of the move. After considerable debate regarding the range of reference-service options available, the staff concluded to recommend to the library director that all reference assistance should cease during the second move. In addition to protecting the department's staff from the ire of expectant patrons, the shutting down of the reference room would allow all the fifth floor's employees to focus entirely on the move for the duration of the operation.

While discussing the possibility of curtailing reference service, the department's staff wrestled with the question of how many days or weeks it would take to move all of the department's collections, offices and work spaces and to set up a reference desk so that the doors could reopen for business. Every participant in the planning meetings had a different opinion on this question, but a consensus was finally reached that one month seemed to be the most reasonable. With this estimate in mind, the department's assistant director requested permission from the library director to close down all public service operations for one month. Not only did the director approve the complete closure of the fifth floor during the move, but she gave Special Collections five weeks instead of four to complete the move. She had, however, one stipulation: There would be no postponing a reopening date.

Next Special Collections had to decide when to begin the move. This was a thorny issue that depended in part on outside influences such as when new archival shelving would arrive. Special Collections' staff began discussing possible moving dates very early in the planning process. The first date considered was November 1998, a period four months from the time the first move was finished. The staff chose this date because it was the time that the retrofit contractors were scheduled to finish their work. This date, however, soon proved to be unworkable because the it did not give the library's facilities manager enough time to order and receive shelving or to work out an agreement with the University's fire marshal regarding the feasibility of installing glass walls.

The second date the staff selected was February 1999. By the time this date emerged as a possibility, many of Special Collections' employees, both full and part time, had become extremely disgruntled with the temporary facility's crowded and dirty working conditions. Despite the grim edge to the staff's mood, people discovered that they had so many small details to consider before starting the move that most employees accepted the need to postpone the move long enough to finish a comprehensive plan. At this point, date considerations became a product of compromise between wanting relief from an unpleasant work environment and the taking as much time as necessary for planning.

As the debate over moving dates progressed, staff members began to compile a large and detailed list of tasks that had to be accomplished during the move. This list became a very useful document to guide the day-to-day work involved in the move and contained such specific items as when and where to move computers, where to place telephones, what furnishings to use in the combined reference room, and where to locate department-wide operational areas such as a mail room, a copy room, joint storage and supply areas, and a staff break room.

A best-possible date to initiate the move continued to elude Special Collections planners until the end of January 1999 when the facilities manager announced that our archival shelving had been ordered and would arrive in approximately six weeks. This prompted the staff to consider the middle of March as the date with the greatest appeal because not only would all of the archival shelving have arrived, but the University of Utah would go into a one-week semester break at that time which would minimize the impact on Special Collections' patrons. This date was discarded, however, when the facilities manager admitted that the six-week delivery date was perhaps too optimistic.

The final date that had appeal was the end of the spring semester which would occur in late May. The University had a two-week break between the spring and summer semesters which, when combined with the reduced number of students historically enrolled in summer courses, gave Special Collections an almost ideal time to minimize the negative impact on patrons. This became the date.

Finally, with a starting date established and permission to close for five weeks secured, the department launched a massive public relations campaign to advertise the move to the world at large. The curator of Multi-media Archives volunteered to conduct this operation, and his work was extremely effective. After first identifying the types of people who might visit Special Collections during our move, he created a list of agencies and institutions that could spread the word to these potential visitors. Then he called each radio and television station, and newspaper office along Utah's Wasatch Front from Provo to Logan to obtain fax numbers for press releases. In addition, he put together a list of University of Utah departments, Special Collections organizations at other Utah institutions of higher education, all historical and archival agencies in the region, and public libraries. Finally, he composed an information bulletin that announced Special Collections' moving dates and plans and then sent this to over eighty organizations throughout the region.

With shelving ordered, a firm moving date established, permission to close granted, and a publicity campaign in the works, Special Collections began to schedule start-up appointments with various individuals who needed to do preparatory work before the move actually could occur. Two key people in the whole operation were the facilities manager and his subordinate, the building manager. Special Collections staff had, from the beginning, invited one or the other of these people to all of the planning meetings and now relied on them to take care of such matters as ensuring that the new shelving arrived on time and then set up according to the blueprints, that the fire marshal was satisfied, and that the custodial crews would complete their work as planned.

In April 1999, as the first truck load of archival shelving pulled up to the library's loading dock, the Special Collections' staff completed small tasks that would lead to moving collections. Two weeks before the closing date kicked in, for example, full-time staff members, with the assistance of the building manager and the computer installers, moved all of their office furnishings to their permanent locations. This freed these staff members to concentrate totally on supervising and assisting in moving collections or participating in behind the scenes work such as setting up the department's new reference room. During this pre-closing-date time, the building manager also worked on having the telephone and computer lines installed, the glass walls put in and the archival shelving set up.

Days before the move began, Special Collections' leaders briefed their moving teams, established final work schedules, arranged for the break room to be ready the day the move started, and ensured that each leader was scheduled to bring in refreshments for their crews. The Friday that all of the last minute tasks were coming together, the University held its spring graduation ceremonies and, as customary, several graduates brought friends and family into Special Collections for one last visit to the department. Following these tours, Special Collections lights went out in the temporary quarter's reference room for the last time and the library's building manager closed off the main stairway to the fifth floor. Then the department's moving challenges began.

On Monday morning of the day that the move commenced, Manuscripts and Multi-media Archives' staff members began to move their several hundred archival and Hollinger boxes of papers, photographs, video and audio tapes, and drawings on flatbed trucks to their newly installed shelves. The leaders of these divisions had marked exactly the shelves for specific collections which made this move smooth and quick. Their staff members then spent the remaining days of the move creating finding guides to match each collection to its shelf location, setting up processing areas, and inspecting all shelves to ensure that each collection was in its proper place. Given vacation schedules and the scant number of people working for these divisions, most of their time during the move was spent fine-tuning their ability to locate collections once reference services began again.

While the Manuscript and Multi-media crews were at work, the rest of Special Collections' staff assisted each other in preparing Western Americana's materials to move so that the Middle East collection and then Rare Books could follow. Here several challenges slowed the moving process. Custodial floor crews that were scheduled to clean floors at night in the newly vacated areas failed to show up. This became a reoccurring situation that put extensive pressure on the library's custodial supervisors who had to transfer daytime janitors to Special Collections to work overtime on the weekends and late into the evenings to meet the floor-cleaning schedule.

A second issue arose when the custodial crew leaders admitted that they had neither the time nor the people to clean Western Americana and Middle East's old book shelving. This forced Special Collections to use its moving crews to clean shelving which set the moving schedule back one week and which caused considerable friction within the department when several staff members balked at the idea of being used as cleaning crews. While the immediate need to clean the shelving was met, the ultimate result of the situation was the resignation of several of the department's employees.

Once shelf cleaning was completed, Special Collections' moving crews started transferring Western Americana's materials to their new location. The division's monograph collections did not have to be compacted, and the person in charge of these materials worked overtime to mark each newly cleaned shelf and then closely supervised the movers to ensure that books from the temporary shelves were moved to their exact location in the permanent area. As the crews moved Western Americana's books, these employees proved themselves to be very adaptive. At first the crews used the department's thirty-six-inch long book trucks to transport the department's materials to their new locations, but then one of the of the workers noticed that a smaller, twenty-four-inch long mini-truck was much more maneuverable within the shelving aisles. So this person went throughout the library to borrow all of the mini-carts he could find. Using the smaller carts, the movers were able to set up a transportation system whereby books were moved quicker than had been anticipated while the care in handling books remained as great as expected. With the work going rapidly, crew leaders constantly circulated among the movers, to inspect shelves to ensure that the materials were going to the right place, and to encourage and assist in the smooth flow of the move. As they worked with the crews, they noticed that a sense of teamwork and accomplishment had started to spread among the staff. One crew leader observed that it was rewarding to actually be moving into a cleaner, more spacious environment.

After all of Western Americana's monographic collections were moved, the crews shifted to the division's clipping and vertical file boxes, maps, and University of Utah printed archives. These materials had to be compacted during this phase of the move because the full amount of space ultimately allotted to Western Americana could not be gained since Rare Books occupied approximately 40 percent of Western Americana's new space, and Rare Books would be the last to move. Moving these diverse collections was quick and simple since they moved from one compact space to another compact space, but spreading out these materials would have to wait for several more months.

An unforeseen and potentially disastrous challenge confronted Special Collections when the moving crews discovered, after moving Western Americana's materials, that the amount of time it would take to move the Middle East collections was much greater than the staff had originally estimated. To deal with this situation, the department requested volunteers from other parts of the library and integrated these new people into existing moving crews that already had leaders and Special Collections' staff members. While this allowed the department to increase the moving capacity of each crew, it did not compensate totally for the time lost from underestimating the work involved. Exempt employees came to the rescue here by working on a Saturday and later into the evenings to see that the project came as close as possible to meeting deadlines.

One unique consideration that the head of the Middle East library requested shortly before the move of that division's materials was that these materials, consisting of separate collections of English-language and foreign-language books, be integrated by Library of Congress call number regardless of language. Given, however, the time restraints of the moment, the Middle East librarian agreed to move the books into the new area by language then later integrate languages once the initial move was done. The head of the Middle East library planned enough shelf space between the language collections to allow for the integration to occur without having to move each collection completely another time.

Once the moving crews began to move Middle East's collections, a very pleasant situation occurred. Given the rush of this move, the overtime that exempt employees voluntarily offered to assist in completing the move, and the addition of people from other areas of the library, a cross-departmental bonding took place. Throughout the whole move, Special Collections' staff members worked together satisfactorily, but the special need to move Middle East's 150,000 books quicker than the rest of the collections caused the movers from all over the library to establish a rhythm of work and rest breaks that gave the employees a great sense of participation and accomplishment. No one had foreseen this development.

When the Middle East's materials were completely removed from their temporary location, floor cleaning reemerged as a problem. The department had made great progress up to that point. All of the glass walls were in (each installed according to schedule), and all of the shelving was set up and cleaned for all of the monograph collections except for Rare Books whose shelving was scheduled to be installed and cleaned after the Middle East move. The department had now cleared all of the shelving in the Rare Books area so that night cleaning crews could scrub, wax, and buff the floors before the library's building crews reinstalled the division's shelving. Special Collections was almost out of time and every delay now was most difficult to overcome. Yet, for two nights in a row, floor crews failed to show up. This was perhaps the most frustrating moment of the entire move because time was rapidly running out. To compensate for this final loss of time, the department changed plans and put up the shelving, then had the daytime custodians clean around the movers. This was not entirely satisfactory but it was all Special Collections could do to meet its deadline which was three working days away.

The day to reopen came all too quickly. When it did, Rare Books was still in the process of moving, many of Western Americana's collections were still compacted, and the Middle East library still had its collections segregated by language. Given the facts that the department had reestablished its reference room, all of the department's phone and computers were in place, and all work and office areas were set up, Special Collections was ready to reopen for business by holding a simple ceremony to announce that the department was back in the business of providing full-service assistance to its patrons. The celebration occurred on the exact day that it was supposed to happen.

In retrospect, the two moves that Special Collections went through were extremely educational. Critical lessons learned include the need for detailed planning that involves as many staff members as possible, the absolute necessity of coordinating with all people and departments involved in any part of the move, and the advisability of completely shutting down public services for the time it takes to make a move. In addition the planners learned that it is most wise to plan into the program the use of Special Collections' employees to move their own collections because both the pride in a feeling of ownership and the knowledge of the unique qualities of Special Collections' materials aid the movers in taking the extra care necessary to handle such valuable and fragile items. Finally, it is good, when involved in a move, to consider the probabilities that even well-laid plans will go wrong and that accomplishing a complex move will be harder and take longer than expected. Patience, teamwork, and determination are virtues when dealing with a grand-scale move.

The Redemptorists: Denver Province

Monte Kniffen

On a hot Wisconsin day in July 1985, men wielding shovels, backhoes, and cranes carefully uncovered and gently lifted one burial vault after another and placed them on a flatbed trailer. The names of the men buried inside the vaults were spray painted on the end of each concrete enclosure before they were covered with tarps and securely fastened into place in preparation for their long journey to the countryside of Missouri. The Catholic religious order known as the Redemptorist Fathers had recently sold their former seminary and grounds in Oconomowoc, Wisconsin, and were removing the graves of their deceased priests and brothers to another one of their cemeteries in Liguori, Missouri. A decade later, the Redemptorist Fathers were involved in a different kind of cross-country move, this time with boxes of books and paper, as well as shelves, desks, and furniture.

The Redemptorists found that moving from location to location was a necessary risk associated with being a missionary organization and that it helped to take lessons from each move to help with future moves and relocations. This second endeavor, which is the object of this report, consisted of combining the libraries and archives of the defunct Oakland and St. Louis Provinces into the newly created Denver office. Comparing the transfer of graves and the movement of archives may seem unusual, but they have much in common. Both are jobs that take months of planning and careful coordination of many people, and both are tasks that should not be undertaken by people who are afraid of physical activity and getting dirty.

The Repository

The archive is the regional repository for the records of the Denver Province of the Redemptorists and its St. Louis and Oakland predecessors. It maintains the administrative files for this division of the order, including such records as personnel and member files, meeting minutes, correspondence, reports from different agencies and groups, legal papers, and student records from the Redemptorists' former seminaries. The archive also maintains historical records pertaining to the order in this region including manuscript collections from Redemptorist-run parishes and foundations and the personal papers from several of the orders' members. These collections are diverse and include papers, photographs, audio/visual materials, and three-dimensional items such as clothing and religious relics. There is also a large library with books, journals, and other published resources pertaining to the order, its founders, and its history.

The archive is situated in a 1930s-era apartment building near downtown Denver, which was converted for use as an office and storage facility as part of the move. The archives consist of three locations in the building. The main archival office is situated in a second floor apartment and has three rooms: the research room (11' x 20'), which also includes the bulk of the book collection on shelves, the archivists' office (12' x 12'), and the second library room (10' x 14') which houses more of the library as well as the reference files. There are also three closets which house supplies. The administrative file room (10' x 14') consists of one room on a floor directly below the research room and library. It has four hanging file units, which contain all of the current member files, the current administrative filing (past three years, or triennium) and records from the previous two triennia. The storage area was set up in a two-bedroom basement apartment and consists of two main storage rooms, each about 11' x 22', and one smaller adjoining room, which is 10' x 10'. One of the storage rooms, as well as the small room, is equipped with ranges of compact, movable shelving. The remaining shelving is open, static shelving. The storage area contains roughly 500 linear feet of archival materials and also houses architectural records and oversize photographs in flat cases. The storage area also has many three-dimensional items and a portion of the library. An off-site rental storage unit houses another seventy to eighty linear feet of material, primarily duplicate publications and extra shelving materials.

History of the Order

The Congregation of the Most Holy Redeemer, or the Redemptorists, as they are commonly known, is a Catholic clerical missionary institute whose primary purpose is to preach to the "poor and most abandoned" in society. The work of the Redemptorists began among the poor shepherds living in the hill country surrounding Naples, Italy, but has since spread throughout the world.[1] What once was primarily a preaching order with its roots in missionary work, the Redemptorists, especially in North America, have assumed the care of many parishes and retreats in numerous cities and towns. The order also has a publishing arm, Liguori Publications, from which they publish numerous religious and spiritual works. In order to have better supervisory control, the Redemptorists, who have their base in Rome, are divided into administrative units called provinces and vice-provinces. These independent, self-sustaining groups are responsible for the governance of the personnel and finances for a certain geographical region.[2]

The Redemptorists originated in Naples, Italy, in the early 18th century and sprang from the labors of Alphonsus Maria de Liguori. Alphonsus de Liguori was born in 1696 near Naples, Italy, and was groomed by his father, a nobleman, to become a first-class gentleman. He was tutored privately, entered the University of Naples at the age of twelve, and completed a degree in civil and canon law by the age of sixteen. He began practicing law and was remarkably successful, supposedly not losing a case in his first eight years of practice, but his career was to take a dramatically different path.[3]

Alphonsus remained spiritual throughout his youth, and when he started to become disenchanted with the practice of law, he made a complete conversion and focused his life on religious pursuits. He joined a seminary near Naples in 1723 and was ordained a priest in 1726. Alphonsus pursued missionary work for several years after becoming a priest, preferring to work among the poor in society. He was subsequently asked to conduct an inquiry among a community of nuns who believed they were having revelations from God about starting a new order. Seeing these revelations as authentic, Alphonsus helped the sisters create the order of the Redemptoristines in 1731. Further revelations from one of the sisters, Maria Celeste, initiated Alphonsus to start the Redemptorists in 1732.[4] The order had a slow beginning, but by the early 19th century, it was spreading throughout Europe and had hopes for further growth worldwide. The Redemptorists' founder, Alphonsus de Liguori had envisioned his institute going to America to set up foundations and missions. It was not to happen in his lifetime, but did eventually come to pass some forty-five years after his death, in the early 19th century.[5]

The Catholic Church had always had a place in the history of the United States, but certain events in the early 19th century led to unprecedented growth of the Church. The spirit of republicanism, which grew as a result of the American Revolution, reordered society and politics in America. The anti-Catholic bigotry, which was prevalent in many parts of the American colonies, was lessened to a degree as many Catholics entered the political arena. Charles Carroll, a Catholic who signed the Declaration of Independence, was instrumental in eliminating Maryland's anti-Catholic penal legislation after the war.[6]

The United States attracted an enormous number of immigrants during the 19th century. Between 1820 and 1920, 33.6 million immigrants came to the United States from Europe, a majority of whom were Irish and German Catholics.[7] With this influx of new worshippers many new dioceses were created to handle the needs of Catholics across the country, and having neither the funds nor the priests to sustain itself, the American Catholic Church looked to the religious institutes of Europe for help. The Diocese of Cincinnati was the first to approach the Redemptorists in 1828 for a band of missionaries to come to the United States. Not until 1832 did the first five Redemptorists make their way to the United States to relieve the overburdened diocese and to give their assistance.[8] In the following years, the Redemptorists found themselves moving from place to place in the United States, going where their services were needed most. As their presence continued to grow in the United States, many discussed the ways to properly govern the foundations in America. Subsequently, after the American leadership petitioned Rome, America became a separate province in 1850.[9]

Twenty-five years later the American Province was divided. By 1875, the continued growth of the Congregation in the United States necessitated further administrative changes and a new province, headquartered in St. Louis, was formed.[10] The original east coast province in Baltimore was firmly established with many thriving houses and members. As newer houses were established in cities farther west and south, such as New Orleans, Chicago, and St. Louis, governance became increasing difficult.[11] While the number of houses and missions in the West was not many, the prospect for growth was positive. Many Catholic settlers were moving into the West so the need for new parishes was a growing concern. Creating a new province with a headquarters more centrally located was therefore seen as a logical step. St. Louis was seen as a more practical choice geographically for the center of operations for the western province. The territory of the new province was very large, encompassing all of the states west of Ohio, Virginia, and West Virginia, and including the states to the south of North and South Carolina.[12]

The Redemptorists continued to grow in the West for many years. New foundations were started throughout the upper Midwest and even began to spring up in the far West, in California, Oregon, and Washington.

Other Provinces

Redemptorists had begun moving into the far West as early as 1885, when missionaries came to Los Angeles. Other missionary work followed and the West was seen as a promising territory. By 1924, the houses were so numerous in the western states that a vice-province was formed in Portland, Oregon, and moved to Oakland, California, in 1927. Under the governance of the St. Louis Province, this new vice-province was created to decrease the workload of the main province and to attend to the needs and concerns of the houses and foundations in the West.[13] In 1952, a new southern vice-province, located in New Orleans, was formed.[14]

Changes in the Air

The two provinces in the western half of the United States worked together with great success for many years, but a change in the makeup of the Catholic Church was affecting the Redemptorist mission. By the latter half of the twentieth century, the Catholic Church was experiencing an alarming shortage of priests. This apprehension only appeared to be getting worse and started to affect parishes and the order as a whole. As many as 10,000 priests left the active ministry in the United States between 1966 and 1978, and far fewer men were preparing to become priests. The number of seminarians preparing for the priesthood, which was as high as 47,500 in 1964 had plummeted to 12,000 in 1984.[15] With fewer students entering seminaries, many had to close, including some belonging to the Redemptorists. The minor seminary in Oakland closed its doors in 1966, and the major seminary in Waterford, Wisconsin, had to close in 1985.[16] The Redemptorists had to leave once well-established Western foundations in Great Falls, Montana; Rapid City, South Dakota; San Leandro, California; Fresno, California; and three locations in Alaska, among others.

Concerned, the elected governing body and the membership of the order decided to act on the problem. With the encouragement of the General Government in Rome, joint meetings between the governing councils of both the Oakland and St. Louis provinces were held to determine a course of action. Starting in 1992, the provinces of Oakland and St. Louis discussed restructuring the administration of the Western provinces and combining the two into one new province.[17] In February 1994, the groups decided that the St. Louis and Oakland Provinces would cease to exist; that a new province would be created by combining the two provinces; that some foundations would be closed; and that the entire membership would participate in the discussion and decisions on the creation of the new province.[18]

Both provinces voted to dissolve their respective units in 1994. A timeline of events was also put into place with the new province becoming active during the summer of 1996.[19] Possible locations were discussed by the governing councils and the members, and by early 1995, Denver had been chosen as the location for the new province. Geographic centrality was a prime concern for selecting Denver, as traveling and visitations are a common occurrence to and from the Provincial Headquarters. The governments formed a Site Committee to study the possibilities of buying or building a new provincial house and to locate a temporary site for the new provincial government to stay while a permanent site was located.[20] The expectation placed on the committee was to find a new site by April 1996, oversee renovations, and have the new office and archives in place by June.[21] The Site Committee looked at apartment houses and small office buildings in the Denver area before deciding on a thirteen-unit apartment building near downtown Denver. The apartment building was not an ideal setting for the provincial headquarters and the archives, but other factors led to choosing an apartment building. The Redemptorists, as part of their mission as an order, require their members to live in community with other Redemptorists whenever possible. This meant that the administrative members of the Denver Province were expected to live on the site of the new headquarters. They decided it was more of a practical matter to convert an apartment into a combination of living quarters and office space.

Five apartment units were to be made into the administrative offices and archives, as previously described and the other eight units were left as apartments and communal living areas for the Denver government.

Time for the Move

History and the historical record has long had an important place in the Catholic Church. In a 1997 circular letter to Pope John Paul II, Francesco Marchisano wrote: "achives are places of memory of the Christian community and storehouses of culture for the new evangelization. Thus they themselves are a cultural good of primary importance."[22] Indeed, the archives and the role of archivist were becoming more established by the Redemptorist Order. Every province of the order had long known the importance of preserving important historical evidence for the future, and the joint provincial councils had determined that the archives were of "primary concern" in the establishment of a new province.[23] Regardless of this fact, the committee responsible for locating a suitable headquarters for the new province gave little consideration for the storage of the archival records when looking at possible locations.[24]

The St. Louis Province archivist was hired to become the new Denver Province archivist and was given the task of overseeing the movement of the archives. The Oakland Province did not have an official position of archivist, so the provincial government worked closely with the new archivist and oversaw the move of their own archival records.[25]

The archivist became involved with the planning as soon as possible, but the site for the new provincial headquarters had already been chosen and the archivist had to make use of the space afforded to her.[26] She then began communicating with the coordinator in charge of renovations to convey what the archival space needed. The archivist used architectural drawings and on-site visits to make plans. Renovations had already begun by this time, and some renovations, such as carpeting in the archival storage area, were not open to discussion. Some non-load-bearing walls were removed for increased space and the windows in the storage area were enclosed to make the room free from outside light.

With the site location settled, it was time to start planning the move. With no real resources on moving archival collections, she relied primarily on help from other archivists and librarians. An inventory of the archival records was created, noting the amount, location, and type of record. In addition to the archival records, much of the office equipment and furniture in the archives and administrative offices was also being moved and a list of those items was created as well.[27] With an accurate list of what was to be moved, the archivist began the task of choosing a moving company. It was decided that the archives of the Oakland Province, due to their much smaller size, could be moved to Denver by members of the Oakland provincial government without the aid of a moving company. The number of moving companies who have experience with moving library and archival collections is few, but three different movers were approached and asked to submit bids for the job. The selection of the moving company was based mostly on reputation and the recommendation of others. A well-known company was chosen primarily on a recommendation from the Archdiocese of Chicago and other libraries.

The timeline of the move was the only question remaining. The June 1996 deadline to have the new site in place had come and gone, and circumstances were present that promised to push the move into the fall. The remaining tenants in the building had all agreed to move out by the end of July, and the plans for remodeling and renovating began in earnest after that time. The renovations included roof work, re-keying locks, replacing windows, installing new electrical work for office equipment, installing a new telephone system, painting and plastering, replacing bathrooms in living areas, installing new garage doors, sanding all wooden floors, and installing a security system.[28] Bids were taken, contractors were chosen, and the renovations and remodeling began in August. The completion dates of the interior construction pushed back the moving date to the end of October.

With the tentative completion date in place, arrangements were made with the moving company, and the packing of the archives began on October 18. The moving company had already made several visits to the site so its employees were well acquainted with the collection and came prepared. The archivist had previously identified rare and fragile items and other items that would need special attention and gave instructions on how she wanted these items to be packed. The contractors moved efficiently: the library was boxed up, the shelves were dismantled, and the furniture was prepared for transport. The packing and loading of materials into the two trailers took two days to complete.

The trucks and the movers arrived in Denver on October 24 as planned only to find the archival storage area still undergoing renovations. Foreseeing this problem a few days earlier and barring any other options, the archivist had the movers unload materials into two of the building's adjoining garage stalls which had been cleaned out for the records. Within a few days, the material from the Oakland Province arrived and was stored alongside the other materials in the garage stalls. As the renovations were being completed, the materials were brought into the archival storage area. The moving company had since left but had contracted with a professional installation company in Denver to set up the shelves and cases in the storage area.

Problems

Even though the storage site was not ready for the archives upon delivery, this was a problem that was solved with little disturbance. Much greater problems were discovered as the materials were unloaded from the trucks and unpacked in the archives. The archivist had anticipated some minor damage in the cross-country move, but the amount of damage caused to the office furniture, library books, archives, and shelving material was alarming. In a letter to the moving company, the archivist summarized the damage as such:

a leg was broken off a teak credenza; the two largest map cabinets are not functional due to large dents and scrapes so that the drawers do not open; two sets of bookshelves have large gouges in them; the majority of the archives shelving is bent, warped or missing paint; and both books and records boxes were packed poorly.[29]

The archivist was not unwarranted in her dismay at how the archival and library material was packed and handled, too. The fragile materials were not packed with bubble wrap and the books were not packed with their spines down, as requested by the archivist. In addition, boxes of archival materials which were stored horizontally in flat boxes were packed vertically and other boxes which were stored vertically were packed horizontally in the truck to make more space. As a result some lids fell off during transport and some of the contents came loose inside the boxes.[30]

A lengthy claim for damages began after this point, delaying the setting up of the archives. Throughout the next several weeks, correspondence, telephone calls, and on-site visits were exchanged between the archivist and the moving company. The archivist noted the damage, took pictures where necessary, and procured estimates to repair the damage. A claim for damages was sent to the moving company and an agreement was finally reached with the company in February 1997. The damages, estimated at nearly two thousand dollars, were subtracted from the final bill to the Redemptorists, and the setting up of the archives could continue.[31]

Lessons the Redemptorists Learned

Long-Distance Moves Need Different Preparation and Planning

Many of the problems associated with the move were because of the long distance involved. The distances involved between Oakland, Denver, and Glenview were too great to afford more than just one in-person visit by the archivist and she had to rely primarily on blueprints and the reports of others on site. The archivist viewed the storage spaces before the renovations were started and had to rely on reports from others on the progress being made. Having the archivist visit the site while the renovations were being planned and executed could have avoided many of the problems that came to light after the material was en route.

In addition, the moving company may not have been ready to handle a move of that distance. All of the recommendations the archivist received for the moving company involved cross-town moves or moves within the same building. Having first-hand experience moving fragile materials over long distances is critical, and should be asked by the archivist. Packing and loading procedures for long distance moves need to be much more comprehensive than moves that take place in the same city or building. For instance, the metal shelving was packed next to each other without padding and became scratched and dented in hundreds of miles of truck travel. The damage resulting from proper packing would probably have been minimal.

Be Prepared for Things to Go Wrong

As noted earlier, the move into the new facility was planned very carefully over the course of many months. Even so, unanticipated events still arose. The storage area was not ready for the materials upon delivery, resulting in the use of the garage stalls. What could have been a complicated and disastrous problem was handled quickly and easily. With just a few days' notice, the archivist was able to make arrangements that lessened the stress of the situation considerably.

Other problems were discovered after the move was in place, however, and had to be dealt with in a different manner. The space of the storage area, which had been carefully studied using the blueprints and drawings, was found to have limitations. The low ceilings, the overhead pipes and electrical work, and the irregularly shaped spaces, all worked together to limit the space that could be used for shelving and storage. As more material was moved into the storage area and set up, it became evident that more room was going to be needed for all of the records to fit into place. As much material as could fit was moved inside from the garage as shelving was repaired and set up, but much of the material, including most of the records from the Oakland Province remained outside for several months while more room was made available.

To solve the space problem, a shelving contractor was hired to fit compact shelving into the storage area. The shelving contractor worked very closely with the archivist and came up with several solutions to alleviate some of the space problems. Compact shelving was placed in one of the larger rooms and also in a smaller adjoining room in the storage area. Hanging shelves were also installed in the administrative filing room. Even with this new shelving, space limitations remained a problem. In order to alleviate some of the problems, an off-site storage unit was rented for the overflow materials and items of lesser value.[32]

With careful planning and methodical execution, moving an archival collection can go rather smoothly. Not all problems can be anticipated, however, and some contingencies should be put in place in case of problems.

Become More Involved as the Archives Expert in this Scenario

Archivists do not always have an important role in the selection, or design, of their surroundings. Administrators, committees, donors, architects, and even contractors usually dominate the decisions, giving the archivist little, if any, input. The physical space and environment in which archival materials are stored can have a tremendous impact on their condition and life span. For instance, temperature and humidity levels play a tremendous role in the preservation of the records, and those outside of the archives and library world may not know what the proper levels should be.[33] Additionally, if an archivist is left out of the planning, certain aesthetic choices may be made that have little to do with the proper storage of records. What an architect or committee believes is a good design might have very little to do with archival storage and preservation. The archivist is often the only one who has the best interest of the records in mind and should strive to have his or her voice heard at every step in the decision-making process. This is especially true at the beginning of the planning process when ideas are still amenable to change and little money has been spent.[34]

The move in question had many problems that could have been avoided, or at least lessened, if the archivist had had more input. The archivist was overall very happy with the detailed and methodical way that the Redemptorists handled the move, but she was not present in the selection of a new site and had to make the site work for the existing records.[35] If possible, in a situation like this, drawings and blueprints of the new site should be made available for study by the archivist.[36] Drawings and blueprints are not a suitable substitute for on-site visits, however. As the archivist discovered in the move, blueprints, to someone not used to viewing them, can be confusing and unclear.

You are the archival expert when dealing with contractors, too. The move gave the archivist new perspective in dealing with contractors. She chose the moving company based on reputation and recommendations from other librarians and archivists, which is good practice, but then relied too much on the moving staff to safely pack and ship the archives.[37] No matter how many good recommendations the company has, or how often it has moved similar materials, the archivist should never be too removed from this process. The archivist should personally oversee the packing and handling of rare and fragile materials and should insist on being present when the materials are placed into the transport vehicles. Just because the moving company has moved archival collections in the past does not mean that the movers sent to do a particular job are the ones with the experience. Some moving companies are very large with several different crews and may have a large amount of turnover. A positive recommendation from a library or archives may not mean much if it is several years old and the moving company has different management or workers. In the case of this move, the archivist suspected that the movers and their supervisor had little experience in handling archival materials. The relatively small size of the job may have caused the moving company to believe the move would be simple and it sent their less experienced workers as a result. If you think the movers are not qualified to do what they were hired to do, contact the company and ask for an explanation.

Get Others More Involved

On the flip side, the archivist needs to be aware when more help and input should be elicited from others. If the archivist is involved at a high level with the planning and execution of the move, then he/she needs to be aware if others who are absent from the discussions should be present. As much as archivists need to be involved in the move, it is still largely the administrator's efforts that ensure success.[38] It is necessary that the people who will eventually make the decisions be involved with the planning early on in the process. The more information that can personally be relayed to the administration by those knowledgeable about the archives, the better the outcome will be.

Additionally, when repositories are being combined, as was the case in the Redemptorists' move, adequate representation and input should be obtained from both parties. With the merger of companies becoming increasingly common, it is not unusual for one company's records to be absorbed by another. In this particular move, the archivist from the St. Louis Province was put in charge of the entire move, even though she admittedly did not have much knowledge about the contents and scope of the Oakland records.[39] When it was time to unpack the collections into the new storage area, it was the records more familiar to the archivist that were unpacked and reshelved. Due to the fact that the archivist was not present for the packing and loading of the Oakland materials, it was difficult to locate records as they were needed. For several months following the move into the new facility, two members of the Oakland Province made frequent visits to Denver to unpack the records, locate needed files, and integrate the papers into the archives.[40] With more representation from the Oakland Province early on in the process, much of the confusion could have been foreseen and steps could have been taken to improve the situation.

Conclusion

The ability to learn lessons from past experiences can be a helpful, if expensive and time-consuming, way to plan for future events. While most entities may never have the need to move gravesites, not to mention archival records, there are lessons to be learned from observing others' experiences that cannot be taken for granted. The Redemptorists used careful, methodical planning with as much input from everyone involved as was possible to accomplish both of these moves, and both were completed with more successes than failures. By looking back at the accomplishments and disappointments associated with both moves, they can be assured that the next time a move is warranted, the same mistakes do not need to be made.

Notes

1. Dan Welte, ed., *To Proclaim Christ Jesus: The Redemptorists in North America* (Liguori, Mo.: Liguori Publications, 1987), 16-17.

2. Welte, 21.

3. Theodule Rey-Mermet, "The Founder: 1996-1732," in *History of the Congregation of the Most Holy Redeemer, Volume I: The Origins,* ed. Francesco Chiovaro, trans. J. Robert Fenili (Liguori, Mo.: Liguori Publications, 1996), 101-2.

4. Christopher Rengers, "St. Alphonsus Liguori," in *The 33 Doctors of the Church* (Rockford, Ill.: Tan Publications, 2000), 604-7.

5. T.L. Skinner, *Redemptorists in the West* (St. Louis: Redemptorist Fathers, 1933), 13.

6. Jay P. Dolan, *The American Catholic Experience* (New York: Doubleday, 1985), 97, 101.

7. Dolan, 127-29.

8. John F. Byrne, *The Redemptorist Centenaries* (Philadelphia: Dolphin Press, 1932), 41-42.

9. Byrne, 113-14.

10. Skinner, 122.

11. Skinner, 123.

12. Thomas H. Cosgrove, *Redemptorist Remembrance*. (Liguori, Mo.: Liguori Publications, 1982), 31.

13. Cosgrove, 72-73.

14. Cosgrove, 66.

15. Dolan, 436-37.

16. Cosgrove, 58, 64.

17. James Shea, C.SS.R., Glenview, Ill., to Juan Lasso de la Vega, C.SS.R., Rome, 2 April 1995. Provincial Archives, Redemptorists—Denver Province, Denver, Colo. James Shea was the Provincial Superior of the St. Louis Province during the restructuring and Juan Lasso de la Vega was the Superior General of the Redemptorists during the same time period.

18. "Joint OPCs' Vision Statement for Restructuring" Minutes from Joint Ordinary Provincial Council Meeting, 4 February 1994, Oakland, Calif. Provincial Archives, Redemptorists—Denver Province, Denver.

19. William Adams, C.SS.R. and James Shea, C.SS.R., Glenview, Ill. to Juan Lasso de la Vega, Rome, 13 December 1994. Provincial Archives, Redemptorists—Denver Province, Denver, Colo. William Adams was the Provincial Superior of the Oakland Province during the restructuring process.

20. Minutes, Joint Ordinary Provincial Council Meeting, 13-14 February 1995, Tucson, Ariz. Provincial Archives, Redemptorists—Denver Province, Denver.

21. Minutes, Joint Ordinary Provincial Council Meeting, 7-8 September 1995, Oakland, Calif. Provincial Archives, Redemptorists—Denver Province, Denver.

22. Francesco Marchisano, "The Pastoral Function of Church Archives" (Pontifical Commission for the Cultural Heritage of the Church: Vatican City, 1997), 5.

23. Marchisano, Appendix A.

24. Tom Wright, C.SS.R., interview by author, Denver, Colo., 27 November 2001. Tom Wright was the coordinator in charge of the renovations to the new site.

25. Patrick O'Brien, C.SS.R., telephone interview by author, 30 November 2001. Fr. O'Brien was Finance Secretary for the Oakland Province during the move.

26. Lisa Gibbon, telephone interview by author, 30 November 2001. Lisa Gibbon was working as the archivist for the St. Louis Province on a contract basis. She was hired full time in 1995 with the understanding of moving the archives and then becoming the Denver Province archivist after its creation. She subsequently left in 1999. The account of the move comes primarily from her interview.

27. Lisa Gibbon to Dick Thibodeau, 15 July 1996, interoffice memo. Provincial Archives, Redemptorists—Denver Province, Denver. Dick Thibodeau was elected as the provincial superior for the new Denver Province earlier in 1996.

28. Minutes, Meeting of Ordinary Provincial Council, The Redemptorists, Denver Province, 9 August 1996. Provincial Archives, Redemptorists—Denver Province, Denver.

29. Lisa Gibbon, Denver, to Dawn Hallett, Summit, Ill., 1 November 1996. Provincial Archives, Redemptorists—Denver Province, Denver.

30. Gibbon, 1996.

31. Lisa Gibbon, Denver, to Dawn Hallett, Summit, Ill., 26 February 1997. Provincial Archives, Redemptorists—Denver Province, Denver.

32. Gibbon, 2001.

33. Susan Swartzburg, Holly Bussey, and Frank Garretson, *Libraries and Archives: Design and Renovation with a Preservation Perspective* (Metuchen, N. J.: Scarecrow Press, 1991), 57-59.

34. Swartzburg, Bussey, and Garretson, 62.

35. Gibbon, 2001.

36. Swartzburg, 87.

37. Gibbon, 2001.

38. Swartzburg, 57.

39. Gibbon, 2001.

40. O'Brien, 2001.

Bibliography

Published Sources

Byrne, John F. *The Redemptorist Centenaries.* Philadelphia: Dolphin Press, 1932.

Cosgrove, Thomas H. *Redemptorist Remembrance.* Liguori, Mo.: Liguori Publications, 1982.

Dolan, Jay P. *The American Catholic Experience.* New York: Doubleday, 1985.

Marchisano, Francesco. "The Pastoral Function of Church Archives."Vatican City: Pontifical Commission for the Cultural Heritage of the Church, 1997.

Rengers, Christopher. "St. Alphonsus Liguori." In *The 33 Doctors of the Church.* Rockford, Ill.: Tan Publications, 2000.

Rey-Mermet, Theodule. "The Founder: 1996-1732." In *History of the Congregation of the Most Holy Redeemer, Volume I: The Origins,* ed. Francesco Chiovaro, trans. J. Robert Fenili, 99-142. Liguori, Mo.: Liguori Publications, 1996.

Skinner, T.L. *Redemptorists in the West.* St. Louis: Redemptorist Fathers, 1933.

Swartzburg, Susan and Holly Busey. *Libraries and Archives: Design and Renovation with a Preservation Perspective.* Metuchen, N. J.: Scarecrow Press, 1991.

Welte, Dan, ed. *To Proclaim Christ Jesus: The Redemptorists in North America.* Liguori, Mo.: Liguori Publications, 1987.

Unpublished Sources

Adams, William, C.SS.R., and James Shea, C.SS.R., Glenview, Ill., to Juan Lasso de la Vega, C.SS.R., Rome, 13 December 1994. Provincial Archives, Redemptorists—Denver Province, Denver.

Gibbon, Lisa, Glenview, Ill., to Dick Thibodeau, C.SS.R., Glenview, Ill., 15 July 1996. Interoffice memo. Provincial Archives, Redemptorists—Denver Province, Denver.

Gibbon, Lisa, Denver, to Dawn Hallett, Summit, Ill., 1 November 1996. Provincial Archives, Redemptorists—Denver Province, Denver.

Gibbon, Lisa, Denver, to Dawn Hallett, Summit, Ill., 26 February 1997. Provincial Archives, Redemptorists—Denver Province, Denver.

Gibbon, Lisa. Telephone interview by author, 30 November 2001.

Joint OPCs' Vision Statement for Restructuring. From The "Minutes of the Joint Ordinary Provincial Council Meeting, 4 February 1994, Oakland, Calif." Provincial Archives, Redemptorists—Denver Province, Denver.

"Minutes of The Joint Ordinary Provincial Council Meeting, 13-14 February 1995, Tucson, Ariz." Provincial Archives, Redemptorists—Denver Province, Denver.

"Minutes of The Joint Ordinary Provincial Council Meeting, 7-8 September 1995, Oakland, Calif." Provincial Archives, Redemptorists—Denver Province, Denver.

"Minutes of the Meeting of Ordinary Provincial Council, The Redemptorists—Denver Province, 9 August 1996." Provincial Archives, Redemptorists—Denver Province, Denver.

O'Brien, Patrick, C.SS.R. Telephone interview by author, 30 November 2001.

Shea, James, Glenview, Ill., to Juan Lasso de la Vega, C.SS.R., Rome, 2 April 1995. Provincial Archives, Redemptorists—Denver Province, Denver.

Wright, Tom, C.SS.R. Interview by author, 27 November 2001, Denver.

Delaware Public Archives

Joanne A. Mattern

In 1995, the building of a new facility for the Delaware Public Archives became a reality with assistance from one politically active patron and a citizen who donated one million dollars for a new facility and a number of other charitable institutions and individuals who matched the initial donors gift. At the time the Archives had about 32,000 cubic feet of records stored in two physical sites, the existing Hall of Records building which opened in 1939 and an adjacent underground Records Center, opened in 1969. The Hall of Records contained offices for the archives and records management staff, a public research room and four storage "vaults" for permanently valuable records with a capacity of between 8,000 and 10,000 cubic feet. In the 1980s it became impossible to fit any more permanently valuable records into the Hall of Records facility, no matter how we reconfigured the existing space. We then laid claim to about 6,000 cubic feet of space in the adjacent Records Center facility. The Records Center facility was about 45,000 square feet and at the time housed about 40,000 cubic feet of limited-term agency records and unidentified materials, our micrographics shop and a film storage vault.

When our Records Center opened in 1969, large quantities of records that had been stored in abandoned schoolhouses, vacant military bunkers and other similar places were brought in and dumped on shelves. No retention schedules existed, and it appears that no attempt to reappraise or review the records to determine final dispositions took place as the records were brought in. When in the 1980s it became apparent the Hall of Records was rapidly filling up despite the presence and very heavy use of microfilming, it became a necessity to review and identify everything in the center using records retention schedules. We compared the records to both agency-specific and general schedules that we had begun creating in the late 1970s. At the end of the review process the Records Center holdings were reduced by about 50 percent.

At the time of the clean up, an area of about six thousand cubic feet was set aside for the storage of archival records. Records quickly consumed the designated space and began to expand, row by row, into records-center space. By the time our new facility was approved, the permanently valuable records consumed about 50 percent of the facility, records-center holdings on site were about 20,000 cubic feet, and we were using a commercial vendor to store another 3,000 cubic feet of records-center, limited term records.

Construction for our new facility was to begin in July of 1997, with the first phase to be completed by January 1999 and the second phase in December 2000. Construction did not actually begin until spring of 1998 and we moved into phase one in December of 2000. Phase two began in September 2001.

Basic Decisions Affecting Records Handling, Storage and Access

Early on in our planning process, it was decided that our new facility would be built on the site of our existing records facility, directly over our underground records center and would include renovation of our existing facility and a connector to form one building. The construction would be completed in two phases. The new construction over our records center would be completed first. We would then all move into it, and work would begin on renovating our 1939 structure. Original estimates were that phase one, the new construction, would be completed in eighteen months and phase two, the renovating of the original Hall of Records, would take twelve months.

It was further decided that during the construction phases all records would remain available to researchers and client agencies with no more than a forty-eight-hour delay occurring between the request for a record and its service to the patron or client. For example, if a patron requested a record before noon on any given day, we could have the record on site by the morning of the next day. If the request was made in the afternoon, we would have the record available in the morning of the day after next. In addition, all records transfers, both archival and records center, were to continue, as were all destruction activities. However, we did ask agencies to keep transfer activities to a minimum. These decisions regarding records access and transfers meant that staff would be making daily runs of at least 100 miles to ensure prompt service.

At the time of the initial planning for the movement and storage of records staff, the plan was that we were to have about nine months to empty the Records Center and that "we would have all the time we needed to bring records back from storage." We had experienced some problems in past years with having "movers" handle records, and staff members were unanimous in their desire to do as much as we possibly could of the moving of the records ourselves. By late 1998 it became obvious that the construction phase was very far behind schedule. In order to open the new facility and to return to full services on the premises as quickly as possible, the movement of records back into this facility was given a new timeline.

Early planning for space allocation in the new facility allowed for separate storage areas for paper records, for security microfilm and for other media. This planning was changed when the decision was made to build on our existing site. Our existing site had less space than our original planning needed. With the assistance of an environmental consultant, it was decided that we could indeed save space by storing all media in one storage area if we set and met specific heating, ventilation and air conditioning (HVAC) and air quality controls as well as followed specific shelving criteria. We would have to store records-center materials in one location, microform and other media in another area and archival records in yet another area. Further, all container types in the archival section would have to be acid free. At the time this decision was made, archives had many records that we had received in acidic containers and had yet to process or rebox. Our early plans for moving the records to storage included reboxing all of the acidic containers before sending them to storage. Once all approvals were in line to start the project, we modified our plans and decided to rebox only items in containers that were not strong enough to be moved in order to ensure that the building would be empty by the beginning of the construction date. At this time, it was still thought that we would be able to bring records back according to our own time table, that we would bring small groups back at a time and that staff would rebox them as part of the move into the new facility.

Initial Planning

One of the very first things we did in the planning stage was to contact everyone who was or had recently been involved in an archival building and moving project to seek advice. One of the best things about this profession is the great willingness, even eagerness, of its members to share experiences and advice, both good and bad. We collected a great deal of information, and there was not a scrap we did not use at one time or another. We are particularly blessed to have the National Archives so close to us and to have been building our building just far enough behind their project to be beneficiaries of many of their experiences and activities. We owe the staff of the National Archives much gratitude for all the help they were able to give. They provided one-on-one assistance for specific matters and were endlessly patient in giving tours to everyone we could convince to visit their facility on numerous occasions. While their scale was obviously many times ours, we were able to benefit from many of the ideas they incorporated. For example, the shrink-wrap process noted later was one of their move- related innovations.

The decision to build the new facility on the existing site meant that we would have to remove all of the approximately 60,000 books and containers of archival and records-center materials stored in the underground records center, and that we would have to relocate our entire micrographics unit, equipment and staff before any construction could begin. Since records were to be available to researchers throughout phase one of the construction with as little delay as possible to the patron, our first step was to ensure that the records maintained in the Hall-of-Records facility were those for which we receive the most requests. We spent about a month creating lists of materials that would need to be kept in the Hall of Records during the construction, taking into account how often the series were used and how much space we had available. Secondly, we identified which of the records going to storage were in the Hall of Records and would need to be moved to the Records Center until they could be sent to storage. Finally, we identified those records in the Records Center that would need to move into the Hall of Records. In the summer of 1996, we spent about three weeks actually moving the records from one facility to another.

Data Collection Process

While moving all the staff and equipment and moving all the records to an off site facility two hours away from our research room, we needed to maintain control in such a way that we could always access individual items on an as-called-for basis. In 1995 our existing data about our collections came from a 1978 grant from the National Historical Publications and Records Commission (NHPRC) that allowed us to begin collecting data on our records in a systematic manner and in a format called SPINDEX that the NHPRC created. Previous to 1978 we had no written descriptions for records and their quantities, locations, et cetera, beyond a few checklists, card files or other collection-specific "finding aids" created over the years covering about one percent of the holdings.

This first grant from the NHPRC and a later grant from the National Endowment for the Humanities (NEH) resulted in the creation of series-level descriptions for about 90 percent of our holdings in the "SPINDEX" format.

Initially, the moving of records in fairly standard containers from one place to another did not seem like such a big deal. We have spent many years moving records around from one place to another in and between our own buildings and we thought our system was adequate at creating and keeping the series description and general locations current; until we began to think through the process for accessing records kept in a temporary facility two hours from our working site, which would involve giving sufficient information to non-archival personnel to allow them to find a specific container on the first try. We, the archivists, would not be able to walk through the shelves in a general area to locate a specific item or even find the staff member who saw it last and send this person for the item. We quickly realized how much work we needed to do. Our existing series-level control of records would not be sufficient for the container- or item-level controls we would need to be successful. Added to this, we now had about 10,000 items which were so hard to identify that we just kept putting them aside to do later or had recently added but not cataloged. In the fall of 1995, following legislative approval of our project funding, we began identification, verification, and, when necessary, series description work on all of our holdings.

At this same time we were asked by the records-storage-facilities people who were bidding on storing our records to define what kinds of containers we used and how many of each kind we had. We were also asked for this same information by the architectural planning team which would be designing our new storage areas. We had never before collected this kind of data. We had always just ordered whatever kind of container was best suited for the particular project we were doing and would then go find a place on the shelves to put the containers. To collect this new information we undertook a very 'quick and dirty' review by walking among the shelves and counting the types and numbers of containers we had in use. While undertaking the box-type survey, we recognized that many of our existing containers were such that they would not survive the kind of handling that the move to and storage in a public storage facility would involve. We began to investigate ways to deal with this. By the time we actually moved the records out, we had made many changes to the containers for preservation's sake, which we again did not document very well, if at all. As you will see this came back to haunt us later in the project.

At each phase of this project, we thought we were collecting more information than anyone could possibly want to know for whatever reason. As always happens, no matter how much data we collected or how much planning we did, as the project progressed we learned that there was yet more information that we did not collect and which would have been useful. In some cases we had to go back and collect the new information but in other cases we just made assumptions, with predictable results. All the wise and wonderful people we collected advice from had warned us that there would always be something we missed that we would need later. I can now attest to this: no matter how much data you collect, there will always be something else that is wanted or something that is needed differently than was originally collected.

Related to this process is the decision that must be made about how much work will be done to the collections as you are preparing them to be moved. I was trained with the adage that you do all you can to a record the first time you touch it because the chances of ever having the opportunity to go back again are from slim to none. However, we in public institutions all know that given time and materials restraints we can never do everything at any one time. All we can do is that which will ensure the relative safety of the records and will make them available to the researcher with some degree of ease. Our move process gave us an opportunity to touch each and every one of our records. To ensure that we did not give in to the temptation to "do all," we had to set guidelines for everyone to follow or we would never have met any of our deadlines.

Gaining Item-Level Control

In 1996 the State of Delaware, thus the Archives, was just going to Microsoft Office as the computer program of choice. That package included the database program Microsoft Access. So, the Archives staff began taking crash courses in Access. We hired a consultant to help us design an inventory database and we began to inventory by container all of our records and enter the data into this database. Originally we created three similar Access databases, one for the archival holdings, one for the records center materials and another for the microfilm holdings.

Before we moved any records, we held a number of planning meetings to determine which records would go into storage and which records would best be left in the existing Hall-of-Records building. The capacity of the Hall of Records was between 8,000 and 10,000 cubic feet. With records needing to go two hours away for storage and with access not to be limited beyond travel time, it became extremely important to ensure that our most often requested materials stay in the Hall-of-Records facility. Once we decided which records would stay there , we then had to move records going to storage out of the Hall of Records into the Records Center and records from the Records Center into the Hall of Records. It took us about three weeks to complete this first move.

Preparation of Holdings for Move to Storage

We began, as noted, by creating a container-level-database inventory of our entire holdings. We undertook this survey in two stages, beginning with the items that were located in the Records Center and were to go into off site storage. After we emptied the Records Center so that construction could begin, we began the second phase, inventory of the Hall of Records. The initial inventory process involved creating data for each item in a series whether that be a volume or one of many kinds of boxes or flat-file oversize materials. The descriptive data was collected on paper by staff working in the stacks and was then given to the secretary and various other staff members for input into the newly created database. This database was designed not only to maintain our inventory but also to allow us to generate acid-free printed labels for boxes and acid-free descriptive slips for volumes for each item that we inventoried. As part of this data collection project, we assigned bar codes to each container or volume. This is the first time we had ever used bar codes. In the beginning of the project, our records storage vendor supplied us with preprinted bar codes as we had no equipment ourselves to create or read the bar codes. During this phase we were putting bar code information into our database by hand. We now create our own bar codes in house and have scanners to read them into the database, which greatly reduces the possibility of data-entry error.

Bar coding our holdings has proven to be a very positive experience in the most practical, efficient sense. However, it does take away the fun of walking among the shelves to look for one item and maybe finding other 'neat' things. Thus some of that old 'personal contact' with our records is lost and perhaps even more sadly a little of the wonder of and reverence for the individual records and even the people who 'know about them' is lost.

One of the processes that National Archives and Records Administration (NARA) used, and we liked, was shrink-wrapping. At the 1995 Annual Preservation Conference, Catherine Nicholson ("Shrink Wrapping for Move Preparation and as Preventive Care") talked about how they used shrink-wrapping for protecting some of their materials during their move. We called and asked them for further information, and our staff then visited to see how it was being done. We liked the process and made arrangements to rent an industrial shrink-wrap machine for the length of time it took us to move records out of our underground storage facility. We set the machine up in the underground facility and kept it running at least three days a week for the length of the project. We began with staff from our storage vendor providing equipment assistance and discovered that this did not work well. We found we were much better able to keep equipment running smoothly. We began by shrink-wrapping all volumes and ended up shrink-wrapping almost all of our archival/manuscript containers as well. This was the best decision we made throughout this whole process, and we are so thankful that we shrink-wrapped so many of the materials. In all, we shrink-wrapped about 46,000 items. We even bought a small commercial table top unit of our own with a handheld hot air gun so that we could rewrap items opened for reference use during the length of our construction and storage project.

The storage facility that won our bid was one that is one hour north of our facility and does not normally store archival materials. However, they were very convincing about their abilities to meet our needs. Basically, they were the only facility that had any kind of HVAC available in their records storage areas. Trying to work with this facility has been by far the most difficult part of our activities.

When we were transferring the records to storage, we were constantly battling to get the delivery trucks to show up on schedule with appropriate staff and equipment. After seeing storage facility staff handling our records as they were picked up for storage, we became concerned about how our records were being handled and were therefore vigilant about working with the moving staff rather than letting them do all the work. We also made it a practice to visit the facility on a regular basis over the four-year storage period to check on the condition of our records.

Planning for Return of Records

The decision to shorten the period of time allowed for records return necessitated a new plan of attack. In order to develop a workable plan of action that would get the records back as quickly as possible, we knew that we would need professional assistance. For advice we again called on various archival facilities in the United States that had recently undertaken similar projects. After reviewing all of the information collected, we found the situation most similar to ours was the move of the Virginia State Archives. Virginia had contracted with a firm specializing in moving library and archival facilities and had been happy with their services. We contacted this company to see what they could or would do for us and learned that not only does this company plan and move libraries and archives but they will create basic descriptions for the records as well. In our discussions with the company personnel, we found that they had more experience in the library-description end than in the archival end. This did not deter us because we were doing our own descriptive work. This firm was willing to come in and do whatever we needed to help us get the records in the Hall of Records ready to move to the new facility. They were also willing to help us combine and improve our three existing Access databases so that once in the new facility all would be more easily managed. The best thing was that they would then take our databases and prepare for the return of records in such a way that each record would have a unique home of its own, before it ever reached our loading dock. Their staff would actually place all the incoming records on the shelves and keep a constantly updated database on all records activities throughout the project. At the end of the project we would get our database back with all the updated locations. This kind of planning would allow us to move our approximately 90,000 items into the new facility in twelve to sixteen weeks. We ended up going with the sixteen weeks because our storage company could not deliver enough records in a given day to meet the needs for a twelve-week project.

You will remember that I mentioned earlier how we tracked or failed to track container types as we were preparing records for move to storage. Once we hired the contractor to help us move our records back in they explained to us that we would have to verify every single container we had in our collection. The exact measurements of all containers and their shelf orientation (flat or upright) were needed for the computer to be able to place all materials in an appropriate home in the new facility. In order to do this our staff working with the contractor's staff reviewed every container in the Hall of Records and then spent about seven weeks in our storage vendor's facility doing the same.

This discussion gives me an opportunity to explain that the one piece of wisdom everyone we talked with emphasized. We must never allow the space planners to assume that the cubic-foot size of a record is the same as the amount of space needed to store that object. People we talked with were kind enough to share their own horror stories about planning based on cubic-foot quantity of records and then not being able to fit everything in the space assigned because no space had been allowed for movement onto and off the shelf. In our old facility we used a 42" wide x 15" deep shelf, placed eleven and one-half to twelve inches above or below its neighbor, to store three cubic-foot boxes. This translates to about four cubic feet in space. Further, the boxes we call cubic footers are not 1' x 1' x 1', but generally 10" x 15" x 12" which is 1.4 cubic feet of space. When you are dealing with about 90,000 such calculations, you can see what can happen. It also becomes apparent that it is very important when planning your shelving to be sure it will accommodate the kinds of containers you have in your collection, not just a standard box. I don't know of any archival facility that has only one type/size of container. We all have some kind of oversize or unusual size box or boxes that we need to think about as part of the planning phase. Some things are out of our control. As happened in our case, we received disproportionately large quantities of oversize materials into our collections while records were in storage. In addition we found that the architect had ignored our calculations and not ordered sufficient oversize shelving to meet our original needs, let alone our increased needs.

I mentioned in an earlier paragraph that we had made a decision to leave the reboxing of acidic containers until the arrival of the records at the new facility. When the records had been in storage over a year, we learned that we would not have "all the time in the world" to bring our records back so we knew we would have to develop an alternative plan for dealing with this issue as well. Following the guidelines of our environmental consultant and given the quantity of records that needed to be reboxed, we knew just bringing the records back and allowing space between all acid-free and acidic containers in the archival collection would not be possible. This was one of the cases where we had actually collected information to facilitate our planning. Our database already contained a field that noted if the record is acidic or acid free. We considered options and chose to begin reboxing immediately, during the construction phase. We began to bring records back by the vanload on a daily basis to a conference room in the rental space being used by our microfilming operation. Here we reboxed, labeled and bar coded 5,177 items in thirty-three weeks by rotating regular staff into the project on a so many per-day basis. This was costly in that there were increased pulling and refiling fees with the storage vendor. We chose this option knowing that as we moved into the new facility, our existing schedule allowed for only one week of closure to the public. This week was sufficient time for our staff members to move into their new spaces, but it meant that there would be no staff time available to rebox records that were returning.

Staff Morale

If there is any choice in the matter at all, I would not recommend taking on the learning of new computer software programs as part of any move project. If nothing else the time wasted playing with the system to develop an understanding of how it worked added greatly to the stress felt by the staff that was already dealing with very tight timelines. If you must go with something new, I would recommend adding to your staff a person who is already familiar with the program you will be using. This person can get the system up and running and help staff members to learn the ins and outs of the program, which should mitigate staff stress levels.

In an attempt to keep staff morale up, we not only had the archival staff working on the records' identification and inventory, but rotated records management and micrographics staff into the mix as well. We were hoping that not only would this give all staff a feeling of working towards same goal, but would help everyone to understand the work that is involved in such an endeavor so that all could feel that they were contributing to the process.

Another issue that had a very negative effect on staff morale happened early in the process. It was the delay in the start of the actual construction. We were to complete the vacation of our Records Center by July 1, 1997, so that construction activities could begin. Staff voluntarily chose to work six-day weeks so that we would meet this deadline. We met the deadline, but no construction-related activities began until May of 1998. We were to move into a completed Phase-one facility in January 2000 but did not move until December 2000. Phase two's construction began in September 2001. The delays themselves were just a nuisance; their impact on our records storage and access activities and their impact on our relationships with our client agencies has been a management nightmare. Since we are still involved in this process, I can not comment further on these issues at this time.

Lessons Learned

I would like to repeat for emphasis the importance of talking with any and all of your colleagues whenever you are faced with a project like this. The advice we received was invaluable and it was uplifting to the spirit to know that others have been where we are and lived through the experience. Finally, I would like to share with you a document we created upon completion of the move of records out of the records center and into storage facility.

Delaware Public Archives Move Experience

Prerequisites for a Good "Moving" Experience

Adequately Catalog Any Uncataloged Records Before You Begin the Move Process

Cataloging records should be the first step of the move process! Before the move process began, Bruce and Dave spent a year trying to describe all the records in both the Records Center and the Hall of Records for the guide. Instead of spending all that time describing records, that time could have been spent more constructively identifying records, and then the descriptions could have been added later. At this time all documentation about each series should be consolidated, including transfer documents as well as all checklists and other descriptive information that may have come at time of the original transfer of the records.

If Collections Already Cataloged, Inventory to Ensure All Descriptive Material Matches Actual Holdings

This process should include noting information about container types and sizes if not already collected. Conservation and preservation concerns such as reboxing, development or invention of proper housing needs should be addressed at this time. This is especially important for items that require non-standard storage measures such as the creation of unique boxes or means of housing records like shrink-wrapping. This needs to be done early so that supplies, specially designed boxes, et cetera, can be ordered and received.

Never Randomly Place Records or Volumes on Shelves

A large group of volumes had been randomly placed on shelves and not identified. This material was time consuming to prepare for the move to the commercial storage site. First, these volumes had to be identified and arranged in order. Since we did not review records well enough in advance, we did not have special sized boxes available. Therefore, some volumes were grouped together; cardboard was cut to the special size of the package and then attached to the top and bottom of each group to create a package. Each package was then shrink-wrapped to keep it together and add support during transport.

Communication Needs to Be Effectively Maintained to Ensure Records' Activities Always Under Control

Staff meetings should be held weekly to ensure everyone is working in a consistent manner. Training should be given in filling out forms and all categories should be defined so that all staff put the same information, in the same format, in the same places. The size of boxes, packages and any other kind of storage containers should be predescribed and quantity calculated so that all staff use the same descriptors and quantity when documenting.

Paperwork should be kept in one specific location to minimize the amount of paperwork that is misplaced and avoid duplication of work. Items removed for work should have signed outcards so they can be traced. More notes about activities should be kept on work sheets as you go along.

Steps of process should be predefined and control sheets with signoffs for each step should be created and used.

Technical Considerations

Ensure that all equipment used for any of the processes is already in place and that everyone is familiar with and comfortable using it. Ensure that all "systems" used meet the requirements of all phases of the project. The importance of this issue cannot be overstated. It has a critical effect not only on timelines but staff morale and efficiency that can not be compensated for elsewhere. Employees should be properly trained on the software that is being used to track the records that are being relocated, and sufficient technical support needs to be available at all times. Help from a consultant is strongly recommended from the very planning stages of the project.

We had a new computer system with all new software installed just prior to the beginning of the move process. The system was installed in the Hall of Records building only. Basic training was provided with no additional technical support available, even when requested, until we were over a year into the project. An online computer was never available at our workstation in the Records Center where all of the records work took place. Database control of records, as well as the creation of labels and control sheets all came from equipment in the Hall of Records and was hand carried to the Records Center. Trying to use a laptop that was not wired into the network did not prove helpful and was certainly not efficient, trying to keep the data on the laptop current took more time than we had available. Whenever a problem or question arose, the computers with the current databases were not readily available, as they were located in the Hall of Records, we lost a great deal of time running back and forth trying to verify that records on shelves matched the data in our control databases.

Equipment for Staff Safety

At the beginning of the move process ensure that staff have physical safety aids available, like back braces for lifting and work gloves for working with pallets and carts, even if they do not think they want them. Enforce their use.

Ensure that the equipment supplied by the movers meets your safety needs, as well as the items and equipment you supply. Even though we offered back braces, et cetera, to staff in beginning we did not force use. We should have.

Dealing with the Local Commercial Storage Facility

Assume that monkeys will be moving the records, not your staff.

Our experience was not like NARA's. We had serious problems with our moving company staff, even though we tried training them in the proper way to handle archival records. We found that the personnel changed so often that we could not keep up with training, nor could we get them interested in what we were doing. We also found that promises made by storage company management seldom, if ever, funneled down to working staff. We were and still are constantly having to remind and enforce staff to comply with the bid specifications.

If We Had It to Do Again

Things We Would Do Differently: Lessons We Have Learned

The more knowledgeable (about the holdings) staff assigned to the project the faster it will go with fewest problems.

Staff should be assigned to specific duties to avoid possible overlapping and duplication of efforts.

Create better documentation: whenever a series of records was completed, a note should have been left on the shelves with the boxes so the next person to come along would not duplicate work. Any movement of records must be noted on shelving and all holdings documentation.

More attention should be given to reboxing items to minimize the amount of damage during the move to ensure all boxes are full; partially filled boxes caused problems.

Send only complete series; send all at one time.

Avoid whenever possible placing more than one series in a single box; use smaller containers instead, and certainly no more than one record group should be represented in any one box.

Provide constant supervision for all activities from the time the truck leaves your facility until the records find a resting place in the storage facility, especially in unloading and shelving activities at the storage facility. Some problems we have experienced: oversize boxes being stored on their sides, oversize boxes requiring single height shelving being stacked on top of each other, flaps on the boxes not shrink-wrapped being torn off. Lids being damaged or lost and records damaged because storage company staff have not exercised even basic records handling care.

Shrink-wrap everything you can, even cubic-foot boxes if possible. It provides added protection like nothing else.

Never send a shipment without all parties having written confirmation of what is leaving, before it leaves (that is, when their wand that records barcodes being shipped is not working).

Two people should be designated for checking shipments for problems. If the item-by-item verification is not correct the first time, it can take a very long time to figure out which item bar codes were missed. Never send shipments larger than 700 items.

Our early decision to work longer hours turned out to be a good decision. It not only allowed us to meet timelines, but also helped with morale and productivity all along the way.

The importance of having or creating good holdings documentation at the beginning of any project like this can not be overstated. Had we kept good records to begin with or had we spent more time up front collecting more data about our holdings, our project would have moved more quickly and required less commitment of all staff time and resources. Our lack of good, complete holdings data and our technical problems were what made the project such a monumental chore, a negative rather than a positive experience overall.

Colorado State University Archives

John Newman

Most archival collections or entire repositories are moved for necessary reasons, and many involve complications. This was true of my experience moving the archives of Colorado State University in April of 1997. The move began in a renovation and, at its end, was touched by a flood.

The Morgan Library building, that contained both the old and new quarters for the Archives, was the object of a major renovation and expansion beginning in 1995. When construction was planned I viewed it from my perspective as an experienced residential, and occasional commercial, carpenter and renovater. I thought that the Libraries' administration at that time did not fully grasp the physical and operational realities of what was to happen, nor, in my view, did they establish an effective mechanism for liaison with contractors.

Some faculty and staff with pertinent experience suggested that essential operations should be moved to temporary buildings that would be brought to nearby plazas and parking lots for the period of physical disruption in the main building. Instead, the decision was made to work from within and around the construction area. There were many clear plastic walls, and some units, including those serving the public, moved several times. In general, trying to run a major academic library operation inside of a huge construction project was more complicated, less successful and much dirtier than the library director and her immediate associates seemed to expect. With a good idea of what the future would hold, I did what archivists have always done when dealing with administrators; I planned defensively.

Long before physical demolition reached my wing of the building, I draped the shelves holding boxed archives with clear plastic. Then, I boxed the entire rare book collection—some 10,000 volumes. From both archival and rare book collections, we set aside on shelves about one thousand items that experience suggested would be needed frequently. Our anticipation was that 90 percent of the work would be done from 10 percent of the collection, and that proved true. Items kept handy included heavily used theses, yearbooks, budget documents, especially the ever-popular salary survey and other hardy perennials. For eighteen months, we worked out of boxes and from beneath clear plastic sheets. During that time, based from what we daily took from the floor, about one ton of dust and dirt did not settle on books and archives. We frequently unboxed and retrieved items for patrons and often added or removed books and archives from our group of actively used materials. The process was successful. I would do it again and recommend it to anyone facing similar circumstances. Before the first hammer falls, box and cover everything you can and work out of the boxes. We used handwritten and typed inventories: one copy in a notebook and another in each box. These days, computers would make inventory control even easier.

An unanticipated benefit of working out of boxes was that we found better ways to communicate with patrons about the advantage of contacting us in advance with archive and rare book requests. We learned how better to phrase the advantages of advanced notice in ways understandable and attractive to patrons. Also, since email and electronic bulletin boards were just then evolving, we found ways to employ them to convey request for advance notice to patrons and to receive these notices from them.

The construction evolved with the delays and confusion that were expected, at least by me, until April of 1997. At that time, the new quarters for Special Collections and Archives were ready, but the movers contracted to relocate library collections were at least two months away from my department. I had been watching the movers for several months and observed that they were very energetic. I did not, however, have a high level of confidence in their ability to handle rare items.

The idea of an attractive new suite of offices and stacks sitting empty for two months was disquieting. In the disorder that characterized library operations at that time, somebody would have found a "temporary" use for the space, and they might have been hard to evict. Waiting in the old facility, that grew dirtier each day, did not seem smart. In common with many archivists in unusual situations, I knew that I would have to initiate action, rather than wait in the futile hope of an original or helpful idea trickling down from above. I decided to move immediately, using my secret weapon—karate black belts.

Since 1975, I had been faculty advisor and chief instructor of the Shorinryu Karate Club at Colorado State University. During that period, I trained over twelve hundred students. Several of the black belts had gone on to found their own karate clubs: many in Colorado. Also, some of them had worked for me as student hourly employees. Their familiarity and experience with our operations were useful. Traditional

Shorinryu karate is rigidly hierarchical. My former students were, thus, profoundly disposed to do their instructor a favor. They were also the best kind of workers—disciplined, very motivated, intelligent and physically strong.

Since this was an original idea in an environment that was suspicious of them, I followed a careful, elaborate and somewhat contrived path to obtain general approval for my plan from the Libraries' administration. Permission to use volunteers was a separate matter, requiring another contrived approach, but, in the end, it was obtained. I arranged for parking, access and building security on a Saturday with the university police, who responded quickly and positively to a simple, written request. Indeed, they offered helpful suggestions and went beyond my original request.

The route from the old facility to the new one was 375 feet, up one flight of stairs or elevator. Prior to the day of the move, I planned and documented it in detail with my assistant. She was very new to the department at that time, but she had some prior knowledge of me as a karate instructor. She believed that things would happen as planned: ambitious and unusual as those plans were. We made a few practice runs, corrected and refined the details of process and route, checked and rechecked keys, lights and obstructions and continued to look for possible problems until the last minute.

My volunteers were scheduled to arrive at 6:00 a.m. Being karate black belts, they all arrived at 5:00 a.m., as I expected. Each was properly dressed for the work and had brought along his own gloves, water, lunch, et cetera, without being told. They also had with them four heavy-duty hand trucks, "just in case." We walked the route, examined the carts and trucks, reviewed the written plan and began work. There were only four men, besides myself. My assistant had no operational role; her job was to do everything we had not anticipated. The volunteers, all of whom had known each other for at least a decade, worked in teams of two. Karate rank eliminated any confusion about leadership. My job was to move oversized items and other material that could not be boxed.

The move was completed without a hitch. We moved 2,036 boxes from shelves in the old quarters to orderly stacks on the floor of the new stacks area. Each box was handled at least twice. Assuming forty pounds per box, that is forty and one-half tons, or a bit over ten tons in the day for each of the four volunteers. Three hundred twenty items too large to fit into standard records boxes were also moved.

An area for snags and problems had been identified and taped out on the floor. The plan was that problems would not be solved on the spot unless they interfered with continuing the move. They would be set aside, and momentum maintained. The space for problems was not needed. Not one box I saw was dropped; not one box was misplaced. I may have missed something, but these were not the sort of men who would conceal a mistake.

All boxes had been numbered for the move (on three sides). They came off the shelves beginning with the highest number in each series, were transported on trucks and carts with the sequence intact, and then were stacked in pods so that the lowest number ended up on top.

The volunteers worked smoothly and steadily, using their extraordinary physical strength intelligently. There was no haste, but there were also no breaks, distractions, wandering around, unnecessary talk or anything else wasteful. We took stock at noon and decided there was time for lunch at a favorite restaurant. In anticipation of this, my assistant had somehow extracted a purchase order from the administration. We returned to work and, thirteen hours after starting, we were finished; completely out of the old facility and into the new one. Temporary security measures were activated, and everyone went home, happy and very proud.

Movers transferred office equipment the next Monday. Permanent security devices were transferred and checked once, as an event, rather than over time, as a process. During the next month, contractors erected shelving in the new stacks. One student employee and I shelved everything, depleting the stacks of boxes, according to plan, as shelves marched toward them across the floor.

The move had been so smooth that the records boxes remained in excellent shape. As the contents of each were shelved, I collapsed and preserved almost all of them. Many were later given to our circulation department, and I still notice them to this day, with our distinctive markings, rolling back and forth to our remote storage facility. This unanticipated benefit was that of a realized savings of several hundred dollars.

I strongly recommend our successful experience to the consideration of others. If karate black belts cannot be found, I would suggest any other group, perhaps a sports team, whose members are physically strong and accustomed to working together. This is not a proper occasion, if there ever is one, for misplaced egalitarianism or false economy. Compared to what I saw of the contract employees, the advantages of quality people were tremendous. Moving archives and rare books is complicated and full of risk. More people mean more human resources, but also more complications that you do not want. I believe the fewest who can do the job is best.

Other lessons that might be adopted are those of securing the building when rare material is in transit and moving quickly—in one day if possible. Remember that my first recommendation is to put everything in boxes and move the boxes. Do not move unboxed material unless it will not fit in a box. I also suggested that at least one member of the senior staff be on hand with no assigned duties—enough will come up. Plan to set problems aside in a designated area, and hope not to use it.

Our move was properly, but probably insufficiently, praised as a tight, focused and successful operation. A few administrators visited us, looked around, nodded and went away—vaguely happy at least that Archives and Special Collections were off the list of undone things, but blissfully uncaring and unaware of how much had been moved how well. And so things would have rested, had not nature taken a hand.

On July 27, 1997, Ft. Collins suffered a major flood. There were five deaths and hundreds of millions of dollars of damage. The university was at the center of the flood, and the partially finished library was at the center of the university. The old quarters of my department, where we still would have been, had about five inches of water on the floor—plenty to wick up the stacks.

A personal friend on the scene called me when the first wall in the Morgan Library basement burst, and I was able to wade and swim the two miles from my home in order to reach the Library by 3 a.m. I checked the rare book and archives stacks and found them, like the entire building, damp and dark, but well above the high water. I remained in the building for three days, until the recovery effort was fully organized. By then we had a brand new Dean of Libraries. As an old-timer who knew the building, the campus and its personalities, and who had been in more than his share of chaotic, life-threatening situations, I did what I could to assist her.

The flood was widely reported in both print and broadcast media, and I was surprised at the number of people, including donors and former patrons, who called very soon to ask if certain items or collections had been damaged. I assured all who asked that our material was in good condition. In fact, I was wrong, and therein is another lesson. Almost everything had been moved and was, indeed, safe from the flood water. However, in the confusion of the situation and in the smugness of having been ahead of the problem, I simply forgot that we had a literary manuscript out for evaluation in a library unit located in the basement.

Immediate needs of flood recovery kept us from performing our usual cycle of specific and random inventories, so we did not independently learn of the missing manuscript. Also, it is obscure (and, in fact, of marginal interest to anyone.) No patron requested it. The manuscript finally came to our attention some months after the flood. After it had been retrieved, dried and moved from desk to desk in our flood recovery operation, someone read a few lines, made a connection, and called us. We were both embarrassed and happy to have it back. In the disorder of a move (or of a flood) you need to be sure that everything is accounted for and inventoried.

Colorado State University made what is generally accepted to be a brilliant response to the flood, and enough crumbs of praise fell from the table for a few to land on me. The single lost manuscript was returned, a bit worse for wear, but intact and readable. Everything else in my charge emerged from the move and the subsequent flood in fine condition. It seems that when you are ready, and when you move decisively, sometimes you get lucky.

Many of the lessons from our experience center around planning, preparation and organization. These issues, in some form, will be confronted and handled by anyone faced with a move. We found it helpful to have at least two people count, estimate and plan every aspect of the move separately and then compare their results. Multiple temperaments and human perspectives applied to the same situation will often produce useful insights that one would have missed. Also, the process of discussing, comparing and synthesizing different views invariably leads to refinement of the plan.

It happened that our plan worked well in all details, but we had been prepared for things to come apart. We anticipated this as best we could with two mechanisms. First, we set aside an area for problem things and determined to keep the move going rather than to solve such problems immediately at the cost of delay. The area was secure and out of the way. Even though we did not need it, establishing it set something of a tone for our activity and removed one item from the list of worries.

Second, we designated an individual, my assistant, with no specific job but to be ready to handle problems. Normally, I would have taken that role myself and generally recommend that the most senior person involved be unassigned. In our case, my assistant had joined us so recently that she was not fully trained in handling rare items, but she was familiar with general Libraries and university processes and personalities. Accordingly, she served well as the unassigned person. In fact, much of her work, which we did not expect, was to respond to persons who wanted to know what we were doing or who offered to help. She also monitored and moved our volunteers' personal property and provided human security at some doors we had originally planned to lock and unlock.

Our greatest advantage, which might be difficult for others to duplicate, was the karate volunteers and their special relationship to me and to our department. Other archivists will be faced with the decision whether to use trained staff and go slowly or employ contract movers and be fast. Both choices have unappealing aspects, and one may be selected as the lesser of two evils.

Good fortune put our process within a single building. Those who move archives outside, or across town, or to another state, must consider weather, traffic, security, and a host of other issues. Planning and preparation are essential, but something usually goes wrong. Then, a bold and determined attitude, applied to relentless momentum, will see you through.

Northwestern University Library

Patrick M. Quinn

In this chapter I wish to recount the experiences of two major archival moves that I directed during the course of my thirty-five year archival career. A comparison of these two moves hopefully will be illuminating both for their similarities and their differences. During the first move, as a real novice, I "winged it," albeit with the welcome counsel of my senior archival colleagues. The experience gained during the first move served well during the second move, which occurred some twenty-seven years after the first. All accounts of archival moves are inherently prosaic, yet I hope that some of the practical experience gained during the two moves described hereafter will be of assistance to other archivists faced with similar, often daunting challenges.

Like most archivists of my generation, I became an archivist by happenstance rather than design. At the beginning of September 1966, I was about to commence my third year as a graduate student in American history at the University of Wisconsin. Married, with a three-month-old daughter, I was, to put it simply, broke and desperately in need of a job. I stopped by the student employment office and, scanning the job notices, I saw one advertising an assistant archivist position at the State Historical Society of Wisconsin, a major American history research repository located on the University's campus. Both as an undergraduate and a graduate student, I had spent many enjoyable hours reading at the State Historical Society and had become quite fond of the "Grand Old Lady of State Street," as the neo-classical building was called by the graduate student cognoscenti. But, shamefully for a graduate student in history, I had only a vague notion of what an archivist did. However, since I knew of another student, whom I regarded as "cool," who had gotten a job as an assistant archivist several years prior, I decided to apply for the job.

I walked the short distance to the Historical Society and took the elevator to the fourth floor where the Archives was located. I told the receptionist that I wanted to apply for a job as an assistant archivist. She ushered me into the office of the State Archivist, a boyish-looking man, who I later learned had only been State Archivist for two years. Over the next several decades the State Archivist, F. Gerald Ham, became a major contributor to the archival literature and a Fellow and President of the Society of American Archivists. Immediately after the interview, which was more a genial conversation than a grilling, I was hired on the spot and introduced to another young archivist who looked like a graduate student and, as it turned out, had been one. He took me directly to the stacks, pointed to the shelves filled with old volumes encrusted with colorful varieties of mold, and funny shaped boxes which I later learned were vertical-file boxes, and told me to "process" all this stuff. The archivist departed, leaving me to ponder his instructions and to pore over the records. They were nineteenth-century records of the village of Hudson, located in northwestern Wisconsin on the St. Croix River, across from Minnesota. For the next several days I messed around with the records until I finally summoned the courage to ask my supervisor what he had meant by "process." He patiently explained arrangement and description and sent me back to the stacks. I spent the rest of the year processing state and local records.

All of the above is, of course, prelude. By the end of the year, construction had been completed on a new addition to the State Historical Society building which filled in the open "U" shaped courtyard on the building's west side with eight floors of stacks. The Society's Library, the Archives' stacks in the south wing of the building, and the Manuscript Department's stacks in the north wing had become grossly overcrowded. The vast majority of the holdings of the State Archives, however, were housed not in the Historical Society building, but rather in the basement and subbasements of the State Capitol building and in similar quarters in the State Office Building, both located in downtown Madison, about a mile east of the University campus.

The rather daunting task, then, that confronted the Archives staff was to quickly and efficiently move tens of thousands of cubic feet of records from the State Capitol and the State Office Building, as well as from the stacks of the old north and south wings of the Historical Society, into the stack area of the new addition. While the initial planning for the move was made by the three senior archivists, Jack Jallings, Frank DeLoughery, and Dave Delgado, and the methodology of the move devised by Dave, it soon fell to me, largely by default, as a twenty-four-year-old rookie archivist, to actually supervise the move. I had no choice but to learn on the job as the move got underway. We decided, given the tight timetable of several weeks established by the Society's Director, that it was imperative to complete the move as rapidly and expeditiously as possible.

The basic finding-aid for the records series in the State Archives was the "Kardex," a heavy metal cabinet containing pullout shelves to which were attached removable 3" x 5" cards. The Kardex cards, arranged by series number within record groups, recorded the essential information about each processed records series, as well as a brief description of the series. The first step that we took in planning the move was to create a blank form on half of an 8½" x 11" sheet on which we wrote the records series title, number and type of boxes in the series (legal or letter-size archives boxes or record cartons), and the present location of the records. We left blank a line for recording the new location and reserved a space at the bottom of the form for "comments."

Next we devised the basic arrangement of the shelving scheme in the new-stack area. The new addition to the building had eight floors of stacks including a basement floor. It had been decided that the State Historical Society's Museum would use the basement level for storage and the Society's Library would occupy the next three floors (1st, 1M, and 2nd). The Archives and Manuscripts departments (which were later consolidated into a single Archives department) would occupy the remaining four floors (2M, 3rd, 3M, and 4th), with two floors allocated to each. It was further determined that processed holdings of both archives and manuscripts would be kept separate from unprocessed holdings. Finally, it was decided to shelve processed archives in record group and series order, processed manuscripts in the order of their collection number (Mss 1, Mss 2, et cetera), and unprocessed archives and manuscripts in order of their respective accession numbers.

Before the move we carefully set up a locator system for the new stacks and assigned and affixed appropriate numbers and letters to each range, section, and shelf (Range 1, Section A, Shelf 1, et cetera). I well recall standing on the fourth floor of the new-stack addition staring at the sea of empty, shiny, new green shelves before me and wondering whether or not they ever would be filled. As it turned out, most of the shelves on all four floors were fully occupied just five years later.

With a strategy in place for moving the records, the next key task was to orchestrate the move. It would prove to be a complex challenge. Because of the decision to shelve the records in record-group and series order, and the fact that contiguous series of state records were housed in three different locations, coordination of the moving and shelving sequence assumed paramount importance. Semi-trailer trucks had been rented to transport the records from the State Capitol and the State Office Building to the Historical Society. The "control" sheets of paper referred to above determined the order in which the records were packed. The challenge was to load the semi-trailers so that the highest-numbered series were placed at the back of the trailers and the lowest-numbered series in the front.

Packing the semi-trailers was somewhat akin to bricklayers laying down contiguous courses of bricks. The archival boxes were placed on library carts and flatbed hand-trucks and taken up the freight elevators to the loading docks of the two buildings where they were packed in the semi-trailers in neat rows that ran from side to side and floor to ceiling. Row after row of boxes was packed into the semis as snugly as possible to ensure against the load's shifting. Student assistants supplied the labor of moving and packing the records into the trailers. The task was paced so that the two semi-trailers were filled at the same rate, despite differences in the distances the records had to be moved within the two buildings and different encumbrances that confronted the move in each building.

The major problems that we encountered were that, in numerous instances, records series were not found at the locations where they were supposed to be; there were often discrepancies between the number of boxes that were supposed to be in a series and the number of boxes that we actually found; and there were numerous errors in the series titles on the box labels. We soon realized that we were engaged not merely in a physical move, but in a *de facto* survey or inventory of the entire archival holdings of the State Historical Society. As boxes inevitably tipped over, fell off carts, or otherwise opened throughout the move, we discovered that the physical condition of many of the records was appalling. We noted these preservation or conservation issues on the control sheets as we encountered them. We also discovered to our horror that many series of records that had been listed as processed had, in fact, never been processed—the records had simply been crammed into boxes. Records series that needed processing or reprocessing were duly noted on our control sheets. Additionally, we encountered many series of records that had no enduring value and should have been destroyed if a rigorous appraisal process had been in place at the time of their accessioning many years before. Most of these discoveries were serendipitous since we could not afford the time to closely and systematically review each records series. To do so would have broken the momentum and coordination of the move, and the move probably would have taken many months to complete. We did realize, however, that what we were encountering on a random basis was a revelation of mistakes that had been made over the past several decades.

It was, of course, with great relief that we emerged from the catacombs of the State Capitol and the State Office Building with the last cartload of archival boxes. The archival boxes had filled each of the semi-trailers to its capacity. As we drove off we glanced back at the two abandoned storage areas, which looked like forlorn, looted tombs. The semi-trailers were driven the mile to the State Historical Society and the trailers were detached and backed up to the loading dock. Now the real fun began.

The "control sheets" determined the sequence of the move. Teams of student assistants who had commandeered every available cart and flatbed hand-truck in the building (much to the distress of the librarians) were at the ready on the loading dock, shivering mightily in the cold of a Wisconsin January. The trick was to orchestrate a convergence of three streams of records at exactly the right moment in the shelving process. Three of us controlled the move. One colleague served as the main dispatcher, directing the unloading of the two semi-trailers in records-series order. He was in touch by phone with another archivist who was dispatching filled carts from the old stacks. I served as shelving controller in the new stacks. As we dispatched each records series, it was accompanied by its respective control sheet.

To our relief the system worked smoothly and efficiently. The major problems we encountered were missing boxes, entire series of missing records, and other discrepancies such as those we had discovered during the packing of the semi-trailers. We simply left spaces for the missing boxes. Before very long the new stack ranges were filling up. The new location of each series was penciled in on the control sheets later to be transferred to the Kardex finding-aid cards. Once we had emptied the two semi-trailers and the old Archives stacks and had placed the entire holdings of the State Archives on the new, shiny green shelves, we knew we had broken the back of the job. Moving the processed and unprocessed manuscript collections from the old north wing to the new stacks was a piece of cake. Most of the older manuscripts were housed in old black "clamshell" boxes rather than the standard gray "Hollinger" archival boxes. The task was completed very quickly because of the relatively short distance between the old and new stacks and the fact that the manuscript collections were in infinitely better shape than the state records.

As the last cartload of manuscript boxes was unloaded and shelved, I stood and silently surveyed the long rows of neatly filled shelves. The "move," once seemingly impossible, was done. I felt what a skilled bricklayer must experience viewing the perfect wall in which he or she has just finished laying the final mortared brick. The pause, however delicious, was but momentary, for we had ahead of us the rather formidable task of resolving all of the issues that we had uncovered during the move. There were labels to be corrected, missing records series and boxes to locate, series to be reappraised and deaccessioned, attention paid to preservation and conservation needs, and hundreds of boxes of records to be processed or reprocessed.

"The Move" Redux

By the time 1994 rolled around, I had been serving as University Archivist at Northwestern University for the preceding two decades. The University Archives was and is located in the Deering Library on the University's Evanston campus where it occupies the ground floor of the Library. Since 1982, the Archives' major storage area had been Deering Room 102, which held about 10,000 cubic feet of records housed on industrial shelving, located down the hall from the Archives Reading Room and workrooms.

In the autumn of 1994 the Archives staff was informed that it would have to vacate Room 102 no later than the end of January 1995 so that the space could be turned over to the University Library's Government Publications Department. In exchange, the Archives would be given new storage space in two areas: two partial stacks floors in the Deering Library (opened in 1933) relatively close to the Archives Reading Room and staff areas; and ample space in the basement of the main University Library building (opened in 1970) which was connected to Deering, but nonetheless a considerable distance from Room 102. A vigorous protest of this unfortunate decision proved of no avail. Reality and denial set in, and I did not begin to plan for the move until shortly before the Christmas holidays. The Archives was given a modest budget to support the move and I used the funds to hire a former student assistant to help plan and execute the work. He was about the same age that I had been during the move at the State Historical Society of Wisconsin almost three decades earlier.

I next sat down and tried to recall how we had made that storied move in Madison. I was aware that the key to a successful move was prior planning and preparation. My assistant, Chris, and I examined both of the designated new-storage areas and quickly determined that the Deering stacks were absolutely filthy and required a thorough scrubbing and cleaning. Janitorial assistance was not forthcoming so we did it ourselves. We then marked all of the ranges, sections, and shelves in both venues with locator numbers and letters.

Then, just to be on the safe side, we placed a standard archival box on a shelf in the Deering stacks to make sure that it would fit. We almost sank to our knees in despair as we immediately saw that it would not. The shelves had been configured for standard size books. We had no choice but to reconfigure every shelf, which was an enormous and tedious job that resulted in numerous skinned knuckles.

Because we had long since filled all of the available shelves in Deering Room 102, subsequent accessions necessarily had been stored on the floor around the room's periphery and in the aisles. The accessions had been left in their original containers, including copier-paper boxes, suitcases and plastic garbage bags. We rehoused all of these accessions into standard record cartons. We next reviewed all of the accession control cards (we had not automated our accessioning system and still used 3" x 5" cards for each accession) for unprocessed accessions. This review yielded what we had suspected. There were quite a few accessions of records that had been designated "evaluate for destruction" because their informational or evidential value was intermediate or marginal. Northwestern does not have a records management program, so we had frequently been compelled to accession records with short- or medium-term retention periods. We decided to follow our admonition and reappraise these accessions, which resulted in the deaccessioning and destruction of approximately five hundred cubic feet of records. Our operating theory was that there was no point in taking the time or making the effort to move hundreds of cubic feet of records that we could destroy.

Finally we had all of our ducks in a row. The planning and preparation had been completed. We borrowed from the Circulation department about twenty-five book carts that could accommodate archival boxes and record cartons, and assembled three crews of student assistants. One crew was assigned to finding the records series and accessions as I called out their location, based on a printout on a clipboard at my dispatching station, and loading them on carts. A much larger crew of two-person teams pushed the carts from the Room 102 to the new storage areas, and the third crew shelved the records and recorded their new location. It took a little while to develop a smooth, systematic rhythm but soon we were running like a well-oiled machine with records located and loaded, carts leaving and arriving just in time, and our new space rapidly being filled. We were actually astonished by how quickly and smoothly the move was completed. It took us four working days.

As I dispatched each cart of unprocessed accessions, I was able to make notes that would prove useful in setting up future processing priority lists. After the move was completed, we were quite pleased to find that only fifteen accessions, comprising less than ten cubic feet, could not be located. An analysis of the missing accessions suggested that most probably they had been folded into other accessions or had been processed without being so noted in our records. At the conclusion of the move, however, as I looked at the empty, ghostly shelving that had held our records, I felt not the elation of a job well done but the sadness of having been forced to vacate the premises.

A Bonus: The Third Move

Since the early 1980s the University Archives had occupied two storage rooms in the basement of the old Law School Library on Northwestern University's Chicago campus, some twelve miles south of the Evanston campus, where the University Archives is located. In these rooms were housed approximately 600 cubic feet of records of the Law School and of the Medical School. In early 1999 the University Archives was informed that the Dean of the Law School was appropriating these rooms for his own use and that the Archives would have to vacate them no later than June of that year.

As our outrage at this eviction turned to dismay, we began planning the move. Upon surveying the rooms we discovered that many unaccessioned boxes of records had been placed there without our knowledge. Some were in file cabinets, others in boxes and paper bags, and some were just strewn on the floor. We spent a considerable amount of time bringing this mess under control, rehousing the records in standard-record cartons and accessioning them. By the time June arrived we were well positioned for the move.

We rented a University van and, over the course of a week, moved all of the records to the University Archives. The move was physically demanding and difficult in that there was no loading dock available at the Law Library and the cartons of records had to be hauled up a level of stairs before they could be loaded onto an elevator. Nonetheless, with the strength of young student assistants, we were able to complete the move without any major hitches and within the time we had allotted. By the time of this move, we had the moving process down to a science.

The Lessons of the Moves

While musing over my recollections of the above-described moves, I was struck by how fundamentally similar they were, despite having occurred almost three decades apart. The current use of automated record-keeping procedures, of course, is probably the single most important difference, but carts are still carts, record cartons still weigh about forty pounds, and locator systems are still essential. Are there any useful lessons that might be extracted from the archival moving experiences recounted above? Perhaps those summarized below might have general applicability, keeping in mind that all archival moves, however similar, are also different.

Opportunity

An archival move is always more than simply a move. A move allows an opportunity to assess the physical condition of the records being moved, determine if any records are missing, identify for later correction errors in box labeling, accession data, et cetera, reappraise and deaccession records that never had or no longer have enduring value, and reshelve boxes of records in an order that might enhance physical access to them.

Momentum

It is imperative, however, that the activities noted under "Opportunity" do not inordinately slow the momentum of the move. These activities, while important, are nonetheless an ancillary product of the move. One must always keep in mind that moving records as expeditiously and efficiently as possible is the main objective of any move.

Planning and Preparation

The most important elements of any archival move are planning and preparation. One must develop a vision of the end-product of a move; carefully examine both the records that are to be moved and the space that will accommodate them after the move; spend some time just thinking about the move; try to anticipate difficulties that might arise during the move or potential obstacles to the move; and devise a carefully thought-out plan for the move. If all these steps are taken, the move will go well.

Appreciation

My appreciation goes to my colleagues Harry Miller, Mary E. Janzen, Janet C. Olson and Kevin B. Leonard for their assistance with this chapter.

Brigham Young University

Russell C. Taylor

In the fall of 1999, the Special Collections' staff at Brigham Young University's Harold B. Lee Library faced the daunting task of moving 300,000 books, 10,000 manuscript collections, and a million photographs and negatives—some of them glass plates—to a just-completed underground addition to the university's library. The reality of what had begun years before as architect-rendered concepts on paper was finally upon us.

Could we successfully move our collections—scattered as they were in a half dozen dispersed locations in the library and off campus—to a new facility? Had we accurately measured the size of our collections? Did we allocate sufficient growth space or would it vanish as vapor as we moved in materials from various locations? How could we ensure security for rare materials in transit? How could we avoid damaging books and glass plates as we handled them? These were a few of the many questions we had wrestled with during the years of planning. As our moving date came closer they took on increased urgency.

Planning

To calculate the size of our holdings we took the sage advice of good carpenters: Measure twice, cut once. Actually, we measured more than twice. During the year before our move, the curator charged with moving the book collections constantly walked around with tape measure and notepad in hand, pencil perched behind his ear. "Where's Larry?" we would ask. "He's measuring the stacks," was invariably the answer. "Again? How many times does he have to do that?" "Until he can sleep at night," came the reply.

There were sleepless nights, indeed. The move was a logistical nightmare. Our old locations were on the library's fourth and fifth floors. Our new home was on the first floor with no direct access by elevator to the old area. We mapped out a winding course down elevators, through corridors, around library remodeling and construction zones into a cavernous storage area still populated by building crews. To cap things off a student moving crew was doing the job for us. Based on the high school students we had seen moving other areas in the library earlier in the summer, we were not at all comfortable with the situation. Preparation, planning, and good luck, however, prevailed and many of our fears never materialized.

By the time Larry was satisfied that he had accurately measured all of the stacks—and was sleeping fairly peacefully—we had a very good idea of the number of linear feet required for current needs and for thirty years' growth. By his estimate we would only need to fill the new ranges one-half to three-quarters full. No one was eager to make another move to create space, so we hoped he was right.

Since some of our book collections were housed in storage rooms, we needed to create a system for merging these materials into the main collection. Several curators used brightly colored sheets of paper (with the appropriate storage locations indicated on them) to mark the places in the main book collection where stored materials were to be merged as we moved. We made lists of "live" and "dead" periodicals, so we knew where growth space should be left. We noted areas of active collecting and allocated more space there, as well. The library contracted with the university's carpenter shop to make specially designed book trucks that would accommodate our manuscript boxes, record center cartons, and oversized materials. We also made arrangements with our book conservators to give the student movers a primer on handling rare books once we were ready to go. And just to be sure we hadn't overlooked anything, we walked and rewalked the mazelike course the book trucks would take. Everything seemed to be ready for the move.

Moving

From the many student crews used to move other areas of the library we selected the best, most-conscientious workers based on our own observations and on interviews with their supervisors. We organized our student crew into shifts that would allow the moving to go on for eight hours each day and we included members of the Special-Collections' staff to provide supervision and assistance to the students. We also took everyone on a tour of the moving route so that each person knew the course we had mapped out.

One of the major concerns expressed in the planning phase of the move was for physical security of the books. We wanted to ensure that books would not be lost, stolen, dropped, or suffer other indignities in the move. In addition to our conservators' tips on handling rare books, we bought large rolls of cellophane shrink-wrap to securely wrap the book trucks with. This would help prevent books from toppling off the trucks in transit and would make it more difficult for someone to remove an item from the truck as books were being moved. We also arranged with library security to have officers number each loaded truck and log it out as it left the old area. When the truck arrived in the new location, it was logged in. Having security officers on hand had an additional benefit: If loaded trucks were arriving too quickly for the crews doing the unloading, the officer at the receiving location could radio the officer at the loading area and have the loading crew slow down.

For additional protection we had a supply of ribbon ties on hand for books with loose or broken boards, just to be sure that these fragile items stayed together in the process. The photo archivist had a few sleepless nights himself, so he decided to personally supervise the moving of glass plates, negatives, and photographs, using his own students to actually transport the materials—at their own pace. This was not something that could be hurried, so we were all prepared to work as long as needed to get the job done—perhaps as long as two months, if needed.

Since we were not allowed to shut down our reading room during the move, it became essential that books, manuscripts, and photographs were available to patrons as much as possible. We wanted book trucks unpacked and the items back on the shelves as quickly as could be done. For better service we scheduled students to pick up books for patrons if the books were no longer located conveniently in the old reading room. Actually, once the bulk of books had been moved, we closed down the old reading room and opened the new one. But until all the books had been moved, we needed to provide a courier service to get materials to the patrons. To their credit, most people understood that we were in the midst of a big move and could not always page their items in a timely manner.

We certainly tested our patrons' patience. What we thought would take perhaps six weeks—eight at the longest—turned into ten. Our student crew worked diligently and effectively; they were not the problem. We did not anticipate how much time loading, shrink-wrapping, transporting, and unpacking would take. We faced unexpected delays, as well, such as granite floors that had to be sealed before we could walk on them, construction crews we had to work around, and the distractions of everyday operations.

Eventually, we moved everything out of the old stacks where remodeling was slated to begin in a few days. Never trusting that "everything" is ever moved, I made daily forays to our old storage areas. Each time I found something we had overlooked—something we left behind—something we forgot. It was disconcerting that so many people could go through an area and not realize that books and office materials had not yet been moved. I could only attribute this to the fact that others said, "someone else will take care of that." Books were left in piles. Books were left in offices. Books were left on shelves, sometimes out of sight, sometimes in plain view. Our entire collection of miniature books was left behind. Constant vigilance and ceaseless curiosity saved not a few books from the ravages of the remodeling crews.

Once we had everything reshelved, we needed to build a location guide for the manuscript collections since these boxes were not in numerical order. Without the location guide nothing could be easily found in our nearly-football-field-sized facility. We got our stacks management students working quickly on this project. As we hoped, they located items that had long been labeled "missing" or "lost." They also found some very nice pieces we had completely forgotten we owned since the cataloging records had never been completed or were misplaced. Moving is not necessarily a bad thing!

Epilogue

While some misplaced collections were found, some found collections were misplaced. In spite of our best efforts, a few collections seem to have disappeared. We are finding some of them, finally. But this situation underscores the notion that you cannot be too careful when moving archival collections. Part of the problem, for the book collections at least, was the fact that a few of the book trucks got out of order when they were moved. In our haste to get trucks unloaded, we sometimes overlooked the break in call number sequence. A thorough shelf reading is, thankfully, finding some of these problems.

Another miscalculation we realized in hindsight was the fact that no matter how adept the students seemed to be, these were not—after all—their books. This was just another job for most of them. As a result, sometimes they seemed to have a cavalier attitude about what they were doing. For example, we entrusted moving an oversized rare book storage area to a group of our "best" students without the oversight of a curator. For some unknown reason a number of books were left behind. We did not realize this until I started receiving telephone calls from our library colleagues saying that large rare books were showing up in various places in the library. I quickly scoured the old oversized book storage area and found a handful of other books that had been abandoned.

In addition to people problems we also encountered a few unexpected shortcomings with our new, moveable, compact shelving. One problem was that the shelving was slightly shallower than our old shelving. As a result a few books and pamphlet boxes that fit snuggly on our old shelves could not be placed on the new shelves. They needed to be recataloged to quarto or folio shelves. Since it would take some time for the catalogers to process all of the items needing recataloging, we created a staging area for this material to wait until the catalogers could handle it. This has unfortunately caused some grief with patrons when we cannot find items where they are "supposed to be" on the regular shelves—forgetting that they may have been moved to the queue for recataloging.

Another problem was the configuration of the internal cross braces running down the center of some shelving ranges. We had designed some shelves to accommodate large, flat-document boxes, but the bracing system, running as it does between some of the back-to-back shelves, prevents us from taking full advantage of this shelving arrangement. We are working around the problem but it is an annoying inconvenience.

Conclusions

What advice would I give librarians and archivists contemplating a move of archival collections? First, find out how others have dealt with similar moves (this book will help). Call people who have gone through the process and ask them questions—lots of questions—about their move and the problems they encountered. Ask for advice. Visiting libraries that have moved archival collections is a good idea, too. So is looking at shelving from your supplier that has actually been installed in a facility similar to yours. Ask questions about this, as well. Especially if you are contemplating movable shelves. Question your supplier about the reliability of the shelving system, maintenance problems, et cetera. Also, ask about safety features and a manual override option if you are purchasing automated shelving. Being able to easily move your shelving in the event of a power outage or mechanical breakdown is important.

Measure, remeasure, and do it again, just as Larry did. You do not want to miscalculate your present and future needs. How often in your lifetime will you get a new building or a remodeled facility? For most of us, this is a once-in-a-lifetime event. If you plan well, your life may not be exactly carefree, but it will be considerably better than having to deal with a constant space shortage.

Finally, do not leave the physical move in someone else's hands. Be there to supervise, to oversee, even to boss the movers around if need be. You are going to have to live with the situation, so make sure your materials are well cared for, are stored and housed properly, are protected from breakage and other damage, and are placed on the shelves in the proper order. Your attention in this stage will make a big difference. In fact, your attention in every stage of the move—both planning and execution—will in large measure determine the outcome.

An English proverb says, "It is easy to be wise after the event." In moving archival collections the trick is to be wise before and during the event, too.

University of Colorado at Boulder

Cassandra M. Volpe

Moving an archive seems to me to be a little like herding cats! You think you have everything under control and then something you have not thought of rears up and bites you. That has been my experience planning to move the archives of the American Music Research Center (AMRC).

Our institution is rich in leadership. We fall under the joint direction of the Dean of Libraries and the Dean of the College of Music. Our Director of the AMRC is a senior faculty member in the College of Music. The Curator of the AMRC collections is the Head of the Music Library. As Archivist I work for the Music Library but have interacted with all of the above throughout this process.

The AMRC is devoted to the preservation of historically significant music archives of Colorado and the West. The original AMRC-core collection (approximately 200 linear feet) was purchased by the University of Colorado in 1990 from Dominican College in San Rafael, California. Sister Mary Dominic Ray was the founder and director for twenty-five years (1964-1989). This collection was strong in primary materials related to eighteenth- and nineteenth-century American-sacred music and California-mission music.

Additions since 1990 have included the music compositions and papers of noted Colorado composers Jean Berger, Charles Eakin, Cecil Effinger, George Lynn, and Normand Lockwood; early country-and folk-music collections of David Brose and Ben Gray Lumpkin; eighteenth- and twentieth-century musical theater; twentieth-century guitar, piano, and recorder collections of George Krick, John and Ann Gillespie, and Erich Katz; and many more. New areas of collecting include popular singers and big-band-era music. This area includes the Perry Como Collection and the Glenn Miller Archive.

The AMRC now totals approximately 1,000 linear feet. These collections can include original compositions, correspondence, business records, recordings and recording equipment, and memorabilia. The materials are housed on metal shelves, in bookcases, and in filing cabinets at three dispersed locations.

The major portion of AMRC materials is on the third floor of the College of Music building on a second tier of stacks in the Music Library. There is only a small book elevator from the second tier to the main level of the library or a flight of twelve stairs. Once the materials are moved to the main level, they would have to be moved through the circulation area of the music library to get to the main elevator. After reaching the main floor of the College of Music, the materials will have to be moved through a small central hallway of the building and out the main-entrance-handicapped exit to the moving trucks. The trucks will then need to drive across campus about one-quarter mile to Macky Auditorium.

The second group of AMRC materials are housed at an offsite storage facility and will be easy to load on a truck; however, the facility is about ten miles from the main campus and Macky Auditorium. There are also six metal storage units that will accompany the materials.

The third group of materials, and probably the most valuable, are those of the Glenn Miller Archive. These are housed off campus about three miles from Macky Auditorium on the third floor of an administration building which has elevators and a loading dock. It should not present too many obstacles except that, in addition to boxed papers and photographs, there are many valuable artifacts, audio and video recordings, and equipment. The one problem here is that there are twenty-three metal bookcases that must be unloaded (of archival materials), removed, and reinstalled in the basement archive room in Macky Auditorium before the Glenn Miller materials can be rehoused on them.

As all of the materials arrive from the three sites, the movers will have to use the front-entrance-handicapped ramp of Macky Auditorium to bring the boxes to an elevator and down one floor to the basement. The archive room is just outside the elevator door on the basement level.

The dream of a larger space began with the director of the AMRC, in 1995, because he had no space to store new, rare collections when they were offered. The original concept was that the AMRC should join two other Centers, the Center of the American West (CAW), and the Center for Humanities and the Arts (CHA), under the Dean of the College of Arts and Science. All needed new, bigger, and more adequate space. The mission of the Center of the American West is to explore, debate, and celebrate the distinctive qualities of the West through the humanities, physical sciences, and social sciences. The Center for Humanities and Arts serves as a focus for humanistic scholarship and artistic creation. These Centers needed only office space for staff, faculty, and visiting scholars. The CAW and CHA have already moved and are well settled in their offices.

The Three Centers Collaboration, as the project is called, separately and jointly produce events that emphasize the role of the humanities and the arts through seminars, lectures, workshops, and musical events. The AMRC also publishes a yearly journal of scholarly articles.

The actual planning for the renovations and move of the AMRC has been in progress for about two years, since September 1999. As the archivist for the AMRC, I became the contact person for our facilities management people on campus who would be implementing the renovations (if any were needed) and moving the materials.

Space on the Boulder campus of the University of Colorado is scarce and precious. Finding a facility took about three years, beginning around 1996, but finally it was accomplished. We were assigned three offices and a large room for the archival stacks on the second floor of Macky Auditorium, a building built in 1919 and designated on the National Registry of Historic Buildings. The building is located in the oldest section of campus and houses a beautifully renovated music auditorium and other offices and classrooms for music students. In addition, the Film Studies Department (Arts and Science) temporarily has offices in this building until their building is constructed. That is estimated to be three-to-five years away.

Like almost everyone faced with moving an archive, I had not done it before. I looked for anything in the literature and found nothing. Next I talked via email or phone to archivists who had moved archives, renovated space, or built new buildings. I researched the literature for specifications for a new facility. I also spent many hours in meetings with the campus project director discussing options and costs.

The three separate locations we currently occupy contain approximately 800 square feet of office, research room, and stack spaces. The new offices, research room, and stack space will be approximately 1,200 square feet. Most of this is stack space and will give us a bit of extra space for expansion.

At one of my first meetings and walk-through of the assigned spaces with all of the parties involved, I happened to ask, somewhat as an aside, if the second floor could hold the weight of the collections and metal shelving that would be occupying the space. There was silence. Everyone looked at each other and said they had not thought about that and how much did I think the collections would weigh. This, of course, prompted two days of weighing and calculating how much the collections weighed. The weight was approximately 16,000 pounds. Then, Loris and Associates of Boulder, Colorado, was hired to determine the load-bearing capacity of the second-floor room. We were not surprised to learn, about three weeks later, that the second floor could only hold the weight of the collections and shelving if the shelving was no higher than four feet. For the requested nine-foot shelving, there would need to be a $100,000 reinforcement renovation. It was back to the drawing board to find stack space that was accessible for the staff, near an elevator for bringing materials to the reading room, and on a floor that could bear the necessary weight.

The three offices could stay on the second floor, but stack space needed to be found on the foundation level (basement). After many more meetings and much negotiating and horse-trading, another larger room (approximately 800 square feet), in the basement was assigned to the AMRC for our stacks. We had to give up a space that was 614 square feet in exchange, and use the larger of the three offices for the research room, workroom, and office for the archivist. The other two offices would be used by the Curator of the Glenn Miller Archive and the AMRC Director and graduate student interns.

The next few meetings developed cost estimates for such things as alternating-current-power outlets per room, carpets, tile, lighting fixtures, fire detection, fire suppression, painting, security, and rekeying. These items affected all three Centers so cost estimates for these items were easy to come by and relatively inexpensive.

One circumstance that affects planning is that this almost one hundred-year-old building does not have any environmental control except the opening and closing of windows and radiator heating in the winter. Accordingly, it was necessary to determine the type of heating, ventilation, and air conditioning (HVAC) system to use in the space designated for the stacks. The historic designation of the building required that no equipment be visable on its outside. Cost, of course, was an issue because the Deans had to raise the funds from outside donors and/or convince the university to fund the renovations. Next we had to decide which areas would have environmental controls. All three Centers naturally wanted air conditioning, but the Arts and Science Dean did not have funds for that luxury. So the decision was made that only the archival stack area in the basement would have an HVAC system.

The big-ticket items now were climate control and metal shelving. It took months for the facilities people to decide what kind of HVAC system could be installed within the framework of an historical building. I kept emphasizing that the temperature and relative humidity had to stay constant whatever system was chosen. This presented problems, I was told, because there would not be anything in the room to generate heat, or "load" as it is referred to; no people, no computers, lights would be off most of the time, et cetera. Finally, one of the engineers learned of a wine cellar climate control system which also had "no load." The engineers discussed this option and decided it would work with little impact on the building.

The next discussions centered around water detection devices in case of accidents with the HVAC unit or overhead-pipe leaks, et cetera. There was, as well, consideration of light filtering or elimination. Light elimination was easily handled in the basement stacks by blocking off the very small windows that would remain after the climate control unit was installed. It was agreed that ultra-violet (UV) filtering polyester film would be put on the windows on the second floor offices and research room. Floor mounted water detection units were discussed and approved. The floor tiles are asbestos, so the asbestos abatement team would have to install the two units in the room.

By early 2001, the funds had been obtained from private donors and the Vice Chancellor of the University so that renovation of our stack space in Macky could begin in earnest. All electrical and mechanical work was designed and installed, along with the wine cellar climate control system and water detection units. These systems are connected to a university-monitored system in case of emergencies. As work began, it was discovered that a blackboard and pipe wrapping in the room were asbestos, so the asbestos abatement team had to remove these and replace the pipe wrapping. All of the asbestos abatement was unplanned expenses. By the end of November 2001, the archive stack space was complete with newly painted walls, cleaned and polished floors.

We have had shelving specifications written, and the shelving contract has been issued. So, at this writing, I am waiting for shelving installation, and have begun to consider how to move all the materials physically. The fact that they will originate in three separate sites and follow different paths through campus to the new facility complicates this planning. The distances range from one-quarter mile across campus to ten miles across the county.

About 50 percent of the collections are housed in the Music Library stacks. Therefore, the move of those materials has to be timed so that classes are not in session and the impact on the library is minimal. The other two sites can be moved at any time because they are located off campus and will not impact the student population.

I would like to be able to move the collections at each site at separate times so that we can shelve materials from one site before the next site is moved. It is, however, likely that the movers will be here for several consecutive days. Thus, everything will be moved at one time. These decisions have not been determined at this time.

I will have all materials boxed and at least inventoried by January 2002. All boxes will be labeled and numbered. I have thought about color-coding each collection so that at least each collection is reshelved together, whether or not in the correct numbered order. I intend to draw a floor plan indicating where each collection should be placed on the shelves. I plan to use the color codes on the end of each shelf unit.

At this stage of the move, with the renovations completed and the move yet to occur, I have learned that planning is essential and that it has an element of futility. It is essential in order to grasp the dimensions and specifics of the move. Sometimes it seems futile, however, because something always occurs to change or obliterate the plan.

One advantage of our situation is that I and the others involved have had time to become used to this process: to learn to plan with changes in mind and to accept changes while keeping focused on the main goal. Working with engineers, other tenants, and administrators has given me some sense of the types of issues and concerns to raise with the movers. While no archivist would consider compromising the integrity of a collection, planning and executing a major move is a good time to learn how to manage the other compromises that are required.

I just hope I can keep all the cats from running too far astray!

Rhode Island State Archives and Public Records Administration

Albin Wagner

Providence, Rhode Island, like the city of Rome, was built on seven hills. In 1989 the building known as the Veterans Building sat like some ancient ruins on the side of the hill crowned by the white marble dome of the State Capitol. Urban renewal and recent construction in Providence has changed the appearance of the area. But then, viewed from downtown, it dominated the skyline of Capitol Hill, a dark mass almost equal in bulk with the Capitol itself. The structure was begun as a Masonic Temple, the headquarters of the Free and Accepted Masons of Rhode Island, a monument to the power and influence of that fraternal order, but the Great Depression and a changing society in the state intervened, and the building was never completed. It sat empty for years until the state of Rhode Island purchased the property after World War Two. The skeleton of one of several auditoriums laid out in the hallow superstructure was finished and dedicated as the Veterans Memorial Auditorium. In its day the auditorium was known for its excellent acoustics and painted murals, but by 1989 the auditorium, along with the rest of the building, had fallen into a state of disrepair. Half of the unfinished building has been walled off. The empty shell still held concrete forms, tools, and wheelbarrows where the workers had left them the day construction had been halted decades before. The rest of the building, which contained the State Records Center and a few state offices, resembled the Winchester Mansion with walled-off hallways, grand staircases that lead to nowhere, and doors that opened into blank walls.

The State Records Center was established in 1952 in the subbasement of the Veterans Memorial Building, 83 Park Street, shortly after the state acquired the building, in half of what was originally designed to be a large banquet hall. The other half under the unfinished part of the building was walled off. As part of the Division of Methods, Research and Office Services of the Department of Administration, it had the responsibility under the *General Laws of Rhode Island 38-3-6(3)* to store public records no longer needed for transaction of current business, but which, due to legal or fiscal requirements, had to be retained for a time period beyond the administrative needs of a state agency. The center was designed by Howard Presel, Records Analyst and later Supervisor of Records Management, with the aid of the National Records Management Council (NAREMCO), employing what was then state-of-the-art records storage procedures and equipment. It became a model for commercial and public records centers across the nation. Presel established the State Records Management Program beginning in 1951. He was regarded as one of the pioneers of the records management profession, along with Emmett J. Leahy, chair of the Task Force on Paperwork Management authorized by the Commission on the Organization of the Executive Branch of Government established by President Harry S. Truman—popularly known as the Hoover Commission—Dolores Renze, and other members of the National Records Management Council, founded in 1947. The Council played a critical role in bringing records management to the business sector and sponsored the first conference on records management in 1950.

By 1956 the Records Center already housed 21,250,000 documents, ledgers, etc. This represented 8,500 cubic feet or 127.5 tons of records. The same year plans were announced to transfer to the Records Center most of the records of the Division of Vital Statistics, including birth, marriage, and death certificates. The Records Center also reported that requests had been received from the Recorder of Deeds and the Superintendent of Health of the City of Providence to accept a considerable volume of their records, and that the State Librarian, who at that time served as the State Records Commissioner, had indicated a desire to approve the transfer of custody of the records of cities and towns to the Records Center. As a result, in the absence of an established State Archives, a large percentage of the records that came to the Records Center were archival material.

From 1951 to 1972, Presel worked under six governors, Daniel J. Roberts, Christopher Del Sesto Jr., John A. Notte, John H. Caffee, Frank Licht, and Philip W. Noel. At least one of these governors turned his papers over to the State Records Center. They are now housed in the Special Collections at the University of Rhode Island Library, designated as the state repository for the papers of the Governors of Rhode Island in 1988.

Presel retired from his position with the state in June 1972 after twenty-three years of service, but went on to become instrumental in the establishment of the City Archives of Providence, Rhode Island, in 1978 under a grant from the National Historical Publication and Records Commission (NHPRC) of the National Archives and Records

Service (NARS)—now the National Archives and Records Administration (NARA).

In 1980 the state received funding from the National Historical Publication and Records Commission (NHPRC) for the Rhode Island Historical Records Survey. This survey resulted in the creation of the Public Records Advisory Council (RIGL 38-3-3) and the passage of the *Public Records Administration Act* in 1981 (*P.L. 1981,ch. 353*; *RIGL 38-3-1 to 38-3-7*), which established the Public Records Administration with responsibility for all state and local records.

This effort was followed by a National Historical Publications and Records Commission grant in 1984 to prepare an assessment and report on the historical records in the state. *The Preservation of Our Right to Information and Documentation of Our Heritage: The Rhode Island Historical Records Assessment Report, 1984-1985*, authored by Professor David C. Maslyn, Head of Special Collections, University of Rhode Island Library—popularly known as the "Maslyn Report"—was published in 1985. Maslyn had been a professional archivist for nineteen years (now over thirty-five years), wrote two grant proposals which won grants totaling $165,000 for the state's records programs from the NHPRC, and has served as a member of the Rhode Island Historical Records Advisory Board since 1976 and as Chair of the Rhode Island Public Records Advisory Council since 1981. Another important report was written by Edward N. Johnson, a professional records management consultant hired by the Department of Administration in 1986. This is an unpublished document titled *Review and Recommendations by the Rhode Island Records Assessment Report 1984-1985*. These reports suggested that the Department of Administration serve as the home for a comprehensive archives and records management program for the state.

Through the efforts of Professor David Maslyn, head of Special Collections, University of Rhode Island; Al Klyberg, head of the Rhode Island Historical Society; and others, Albin Wagner, was hired in March 1987 as the first Public Records Administrator to implement the *Public Records Act of 1981* and the proposals of the "Maslyn Report" of 1985.

Wagner had been the first City Archivist for the City of Providence from 1978 to 1980, had organized the first archives and records management program for the city, and had also held archives and records management positions at Harvard University, Harvard Business School, the University of Colorado, Cornell University, and the Wyoming State Archives.

Under Wagner's direction, the Public Records Administration instituted retention schedules for the records of state and local government agencies, published *Local Records Manual* (1987) and *State Records Manual* (1987), offered a series of workshops on records management in cooperation with the Office of Training and Development and the Rhode Island Association of Town and City Clerks. It also promulgated standards for microfilming records per *RIGL 38-3-5.1*, and established the Central Micrographics Services for state and local agencies per *RIGL 38-3-5(5)*, a microfilm training program in the women's state prison as part of the Prison Industries, a Forms Management Center per *RIGL 42-82 and 42-82.1*, and the Rhode Island Book Bindery and Document Conservation Center (RIBDOCC) per *RIGL 38-3-5(3)*, under the direction of by Robert Chase, formerly head of the Document Distribution Center in the State House and the City Archivist of Providence. A major project was begun with the state courts to consolidate and redesign all the forms used by the Supreme Court, Superior and District courts, and the Family Court. The Public Records Administration Rotary Fund was established to fund the operation of the State Records Center and other services of the Public Records Administration and an automated accounting system was created for billing state agencies and municipalities.

The new Public Records Administrator soon determined the State Record Center and the Veterans Memorial Building did not have space or facilities adequate to service the backlog of inactive records in state offices, even after a reevaluation of the retention schedules for the records of many of the state agencies and a purge of records in the Records Center past the retention schedules. The situation was even more critical due to the pending completion of a new Department of Administration Building, One Capitol Hill, late in 1989, which would require storage of all inactive records of the department in the State Records Center.

In a concept paper for a new Rhode Island State Records Center, prepared in 1988, Wagner stated,

> The State Records Center is currently filled to capacity. For several years now, the center has been unable to store any additional records for state agencies except when records currently stored there have reached the end of their retention period so they can be destroyed to make room for new records. The building, which is partially unfinished, has serious environmental problems including asbestos, water seepage, and vermin which would require a very considerable outlay of capital funds for renovation of the building.

Various proposals were put forth for a new facility for the State Records Center and a new State Archives, perhaps in conjunction with the Rhode Island Historical Society which also needed more storage space for their collections. Renovation of several historic properties in the City of Providence was considered, including the Cranston Street Armory and several empty downtown department stores. Feasibility studies were conducted on at least two of these buildings, the Armory and Shepard's Department Store, but none of the plans materialized. As a temporary measure, space was leased in the Matrix Building, One Catamore Boulevard, East Providence as an annex to the State Records Center to house the new Rhode Island Book Bindery and Document Conservation Center and to provide additional space for records storage when the Department of Administration was scheduled to move into the new Administration Building in late 1989.

On June 8, 1989, a fire broke out in the Veterans Memorial Building. Later investigations found the fire was set in four different areas of the building in hallways and back rooms outside the Records Center. A former employee, a stagehand for the Veterans Memorial Auditorium who had been fired by the Building Manager, was said to be the primary suspect, but no arrests were ever made. Ironically, a major renovation of the Veterans Memorial Building, including removal of asbestos in the edifice, was due to begin only a few days after the fire took place. Due to the condition of the building, fire drills had been conducted there on a regular basis. As a result, when the fire alarms went off the employees of the State Records Center were sent out of the building, and Albin Wagner remained in the Records Center to open the doors for the Fire Department as they toured the building. When Wagner noticed smoke from the fire high above the subbasement where the Records Center was located, he started to climb the round of stairs that lead to the street. On one of the mezzanines overlooking the Records Center below, he saw flames leaping over a "firewall" separating the Records Center from the rest of the building that did not reach the ceiling, dropping sparks onto records boxes containing state income tax records. He returned to his office to get a fire extinguisher to put out the fire on the burning boxes. When he had emptied the fire extinguisher on the burning boxes, he continued on out to the street where he found firemen from several fire companies. They had been unable to find the origin of the fire due to the mazelike character of the structure. Wagner reentered the building with the firemen to show them how to reach the locations of the fire which was then successfully contained, although several firemen suffered from smoke inhalation. Unfortunately, during the course of fighting the fire, some of the records in the State Records Center got wet. Worst of all, the asbestos pipe and duct insulation high above the Records Center was disturbed by the force of the fire hoses, leaving the Records Center badly contaminated with loose chunks of asbestos material and a thin layer of asbestos fibers which had fallen down onto thousands of cardboard records-center boxes on the rows and rows of open shelving below.

By coincidence the Public Records Administration had recently drafted a Disaster Recovery Plan for the State Records Center and had begun contacting vendors to implement the plan. Albin Wagner had begun negotiations with Harvey Swartz, President of Capital Records Management Services, who approximately eight months before had begun renovation of the former Capital Moving and Storage facility, originally the old Hanley Brewery, as a commercial records center. Wagner had proposed that the commercial records center nearby, at 431 Harris Avenue, could serve as a "hot site" where the State Records Center could be moved in case of a disaster. Contact information was also being compiled for supplies and equipment needed for disaster recovery for state and local government records and a disaster response team was being organized. No one expected that the State Records Center, itself, would be the first recipient of that aid. In fact several Public Records Administration staff members were scheduled to attend a seminar in Boston on disaster planning and recovery. They had to call to say that they would not be able to attend since there had been a fire in the Rhode Island State Records Center. Later they were told that their call had made the seminar a great success.

As recent events on September 11, 2001, have demonstrated, it is difficult to plan for the unexpected. As luck would have it, Paul Zastro, the long-time supervisor of the State Records Center was out on extended sick leave, and the Director of the Department of Administration, and William (Bill) Dugan Jr., head of Central Services, were out of town when the fire occurred. All of which complicated the process of organizing a timely response to the disaster.

Following the fire on June 8, 1989, Capital Records Management was hired by the state of Rhode Island to remove, transport, rebox, catalog, and store over 45,000 boxes of records from the State Records Center which had suffered fire and water damage. The same day that the fire was put out, the Public Records Administrator, Albin Wagner and Harvey Swartz, President of Capital Records Management, entered the Veterans Memorial Building with permission of the Fire Marshall to inspect the records. Upon inspection they discovered a fine powder of asbestos fibers covering the tops many of the boxes. When the state of Rhode Island was notified of this, it immediately sealed off the building. In a dramatic scene, while several television crews and reporters prepared to tour the fire damaged building, state officials from the Rhode Island Department of Health marched in and announced that the building was closed. No one was allowed to enter the building due to the asbestos. This created a crisis situation for the Public Records

Administration. It was critical that the wet records in the Records Center be removed and frozen in order to prevent the growth of mold and mildew which would damage or destroy the records: Remember this was in June in Rhode Island. Time was of the essence. Any delay could result in the loss of a considerable volume of public records.

A licensed asbestos-removal firm was found that was currently working under a state contract for a small asbestos abatement project for a state agency. (I believe the project involved cutting a door in the foundation of the Department of Transportation Building that would disturb some asbestos material.) The contract was used to obtain immediate assistance with the situation at the State Records Center, and work there was simply added on to the existing contract.

At approximately 1:00 p.m. on June 9, 1989, a call was placed by Albin Wagner, Public Records Administrator, to International Asbestos Removal Inc., 84 Broad Street, Pawtucket, Rhode Island to respond to the incident at the Veterans Memorial Building. Paul M. Nappa and other staff members of International Asbestos Removal Inc. responded at approximately 1:30 p.m. and met with Daniel DeDentro, Deputy Building Commissioner; Donna E. Fransisco, Building Superintendent; and Albin Wagner. A walk-through of the building was conducted and conditions were noted.

By 2:00 p.m. International Asbestos Removal responded with a crew to secure the area. This company took control of the State Records Center and obtained one million dollars in liability insurance for the project. At this point an effort was made to coordinate activities between Albin Wagner, Capital Records Management, and International Asbestos Removal and to start to identify the records prioritized as to the order in which they were to be removed.

Tests conducted by an independent firm, Rhode Island Analytical Laboratories, Inc. in North Providence, from June 9 to June 20, 1989, determined the State Records Center should be classified as a grossly exposed area. A request was filed immediately with the Rhode Island Department of Health, Division of Occupational Health and Radiation Control for permission to conduct an emergency asbestos abatement project. Asbestos abatement is any activity involving the removal, encapsulation, enclosure, renovation, repair, demolition or other disturbance of friable asbestos-containing materials. Any building owner who intends to conduct an asbestos abatement project must submit an asbestos abatement plan and must not proceed with the project until the plan has been reviewed and written approval has been received by the appropriate state or federal agency. In the absence of an approved asbestos abatement plan, permission can be granted only to prevent personnel injury or property damage.

Asbestos is a unique group of naturally occurring minerals that separate into fibers of high tensile strength that are resistant to heat, wear, and chemicals. It is used in insulation, textiles, paper, cement sheets, floor tiles, ceiling tiles, wall covering, decorations, coating, sealants, concrete pipes, and reinforced plastics and other compounds. The characteristics of asbestiform materials are described in the publication entitled *Non Occupational Health Risks of Abestiform Fibers*, published jointly in 1984 by the Committee on Non Occupational Health Risks of Abestiform Fibers, the Board of Toxicology and Health Hazards of the Commission on Life Sciences of the National Research Council, the United States Environmental Protection Agency (EPA) and the National Academy of Science, National Academy of Science Press, Washington, DC.

In this case it was crucial that action be taken immediately to save water-damaged records and to prevent the advent of mold and mildew which destroy the records. An emergency asbestos removal project requires that a building owner notify the agency no later than one working day following the beginning of an emergency abatement project, of the name of the asbestos removal contractor engaged in the work, the amount of asbestos-containing material, and the expected length of the project. Only a licensed asbestos removal contractor can conduct all of the work. Within ten working days of the completion of the project, the building owner must submit a complete written report along with adequate documentation concerning the areas abated, the amount of asbestos-containing material removed, specific work procedures followed during the abatement process, the results of air testing, receipts for disposal of asbestos material removed, and any other information the agency may request.

International Asbestos Removal immediately erected critical barriers of polyethylene sheeting to isolate contaminated areas from uncontaminated areas. Wall sheeting consisted of two layers of 4-mil polyethylene sheeting. Floor sheeting consisted of two layers of 6-mil polyethylene sheeting which had to extend at least twelve inches up the side of walls. All openings or penetrations between the work area and uncontaminated areas had to be sealed, including windows, doorways, elevator shafts, corridor entrances, drains, ducts, grills, grates, diffusers, and skylights. Negative air pressure had to be created in the contaminated area using negative pressure ventilation units with high efficiency particulate (HEPA) filtration in sufficient numbers to provide one workplace air change every fifteen minutes with exhaust to the outside of the building. The equipment had to be operated continuously from the time of the barrier construction until the final acceptable clearance air-monitoring results were obtained. All heating, ventilation, and air conditioning (HVAC) equipment in or passing through the contaminated area had to be shut down and locked out. All intake and exhaust openings, as well as any seams in system components, had to be sealed with 6-mil polyethylene sheeting and duct tape. All filters had to be replaced at the conclusion of the abatement project and disposed of as asbestos waste. An air lock system was installed for movement of personnel and material in and out of the contaminated area to reduce asbestos fiber migration to outside the controlled area. Airlocks, much like those on a space station, were tunnels constructed of polyethylene sheeting with access though double sets of doorways protected by two overlapping sheets of polyethylene in accordance with the regulations of Occupational Health and Safety Administration (OSHA) of the United States Department of Labor, specifically *29 CFR 1926.58(j)*. A worker decontamination enclosure system, consisting of a clean room, shower room, and equipment room, also had to be constructed and separated from each other and the work area by airlocks. Warning signs were also posted around the building in accordance with OSHA *29 CFR 1926.58(k)* at all approaches to any location where airborne fiber levels could be expected to exceed the Indoor Non-Occupational Air Exposure Standard. In addition, warning signs were posted elsewhere in the Veterans Memorial Auditorium to advise the public of the locations within the building where an asbestos abatement activity was in progress.

Clean up procedures using HEPA vacuuming and wet cleaning techniques were followed. Wet cleaning was followed by HEPA vacuuming after surfaces had been allowed to dry. The sequence of wet cleaning and vacuuming was repeated at twenty-four-hour intervals until no visible residue was observed. Asbestos waste had to be placed in impermeable containers for disposal. Metal or fiber drums with locking ring-type tops were used for asbestos waste containing sharp edges. Securely sealed double polyethylene bags of at least 6-mil thickness were used for cardboard boxes, paper, and other asbestos-contaminated material. Any asbestos-waste material too large for containers had to be removed intact and wrapped in two layers of 6-mil polyethylene sheeting secured with tape. All containers, bags, drums, and large wrapped material had to be clearly labeled as asbestos waste material in accordance with OSHA *29 CFR 1926.58(k)* or EPA *40 CFR 61.152* regulations. Storage of asbestos waste containers awaiting transportation to an authorized disposal facility had to be in a secure location to prevent access by unauthorized personnel. Decontamination efforts concentrated at first on the high priority records, those on the mezzanine, and water-damaged records that would require immediate attention in order for the restoration process to the successful.

Once the records were initially decontaminated, they were loaded on to a refrigeration (or "reefer") truck to limit further damage from moisture. Capital Records Management contracted with the trucking company to transport the records to their facility. The most severely water-damaged records had to be frozen and stored in the refrigerated trailers.

Just the movement of approximately 45,000 boxes out of the Records Center presented a problem. The Records Center was three stories below street level, and there was no loading dock. Initially, the boxes were passed hand to hand like a bucket brigade up the steps by Public Records Administration and Capital Records Management staff members. That problem was solved by the rental of a series of motorized conveyor belts which carried the boxes up out of the Records Center to the trucks parked on the street.

All work practices had to be established and performed in accordance with *Rhode Island Rules and Regulations for Asbestos Control R.23-24.5-ASB,* January 1986, as amended. These rules and regulations were promulgated by the Rhode Island Department of Health, Division of Occupational Health and Radiation Control, pursuant to the authority conferred *Section 23-24. 5-5(c)* of the *General Laws of the State of Rhode Island,* 1956, as amended and were established for the purposes of adopting standards for asbestos control to implement the provisions of the *Rhode Island Asbestos Abatement Act (Title 23, Chapter 24.5 of the General Laws). The Rules and Regulations for Asbestos Control* were amended in October 1988 for the purpose of adopting regulations consistent with the *Federal Asbestos Hazard Emergency Response Act (AHERA)* regulations *(15 CFR 763.80-763.99)* and amendments by the Rhode Island legislature to *Chapter 23-24.5* of the *General Laws* to clarify existing regulations and to adopt a fee schedule for the implementation of the statutory provisions of the Asbestos Abatement Act.

All asbestos removal workers were required by the state of Rhode Island to complete a thirty-two-hour training program. All employees were required to obtain a respirator fit test conducted by a Certified Industrial Hygienist and to receive special training in the use and maintenance of respirators. The asbestos removal workers had to undergo periodic medical testing. While on the job, they had to work wearing a full-face respirator and a set of protective clothing which looks like a space suit that covered the whole body. When Public Records Administration personnel or others were allowed to enter the containment area, they also had to wear a respirator and the same protective gear.

The limited access to the records in the State Records Center created a serious problem for the Public Records Administration. It was not only that the records could not be referenced or retrieved by the agencies that stored them in there, but it created grave problems for maintaining intellectual control and identity of the records as they were removed from the shelves and reboxed by workers unfamiliar with—or even insensitive to—the need to maintain documentation on the records being moved and for copying the information on the boxes identifying their contents. This problem was finally solved by having two of our staff undergo the thirty-two-hour training course and other requirements to become Certified Asbestos Removal Workers. Due to the liability and insurance requirements, they had to be hired by the contractor, International Asbestos Removal, in order to work along with the other asbestos removal workers inside the containment area to direct and control the movement of records and maintain the identity.

In the beginning of the project, problems also developed concerning billing the state by International Asbestos Removal. Bills were not itemized and the number of workers and their hours seemed excessive and could not be verified. As a result, the Building Superintendent, Donna E. Francisco, was instructed to keep and maintain a log of all workers and other personnel as they entered and left the Veterans Memorial Building. The log was also deemed necessary in case of any liability the state might incur due to the asbestos abatement project.

Fine cleaning and decontamination continued utilizing established methodology until June 20, 1989, when decontamination of all areas of initial concern was completed. Air quality reports showed asbestos fiber concentration within acceptable limits for reoccupation as denoted in the *Rules and Regulations on Asbestos Control*. It was noted when International Asbestos Removal Inc. ceased operations at this time that the atmosphere was in a state of high humidity, so asbestos fiber release could still pose a problem once the area continued to dry. As a result, the area was kept secure.

At that point, several nationally known disaster recovery firms and licensed asbestos abatement companies were contacted about taking over the asbestos abatement project. At least one large company made a site visit. The state was told that it would be impossible to take over the project, even if another containment area was built around the one constructed by International Asbestos Removal, and that the company could not assume liability for a project begun by another firm. As a result, the state was forced to stay with the contractor, who they thought they had hired temporarily in order to get the project started quickly.

On June 23, 1989, a site survey was performed with the Building Superintendent. It was noted that a significant drop in humidity had allowed the asbestos-containing material, specifically the remaining duct insulation which was in poor condition, to dry, releasing asbestos fiber, causing additional physical contamination of the area. It was determined at that point to prevent any further fiber migration and effectively limit any liability of the state of Rhode Island due to any possible exposure to asbestos. The area was resecured and subjected to negative air pressure to control asbestos fiber migration. It was also noted at this time that access to the State Records Center should be limited to qualified licensed-competent persons as defined in *R. I. Rules and Regulations on Asbestos Control.* It was also noted that in order to ensure that no liability was incurred by the state of Rhode Island, state employees and others trained in proper handling procedures could access the records beyond the containment area only after the records had been decontaminated. To institute this plan several procedures were established:

Phase One: Workers are to access State Records Center, which is subjected to a negative air pressure to contain airborne contamination, through an airlock access panel. Workers are directed by the Records Manager as to what records are to be removed. Exterior surfaces of the boxes are HEPA-vacuumed and wet-wiped to minimize fiber release. Boxes are then removed from the State Records Center and prepared for shipment to the Capital Records Management Center, Harris Avenue, Providence, Rhode Island. The same procedure is followed when accessing storage cabinets, file cabinets, and other miscellaneous storage containers.

Phase Two: Records are delivered to the Capital Records Management Center. Boxes are off-loaded directly into a decontamination facility. A portion of the loading dock is sealed off with polyethylene sheeting, with access through an airlock system similar to that constructed at the State Records Center. Negative air pressure is maintained within the decontamination facility by air handling units. In this controlled environment the boxes are opened and the contents are HEPA-vacuumed by certified asbestos removal workers wearing the same protective clothing and respirators. The records are then moved out the containment area through a series of airlocks and custody is returned to Records Management, where the records are cataloged and placed in new records center boxes. The original containers are dismantled and packaged for proper disposal as asbestos waste and transferred to an EPA-approved asbestos disposal site, along with all manifests and chain of custody forms, resulting in certified disposal receipts. Wet or damp records are placed on bread racks on open records-center shelving in an adjoining area, which the staff came to call the "Arizona Room," where large air handling units keep the atmosphere hot and dry to absorb any moisture from the paper records. Once the records are reboxed and cataloged, they are moved to one of the storage areas in the Capital Records Management's commercial records center in that building.

This process had been previously outlined and submitted to the proper authorities involved in this project, along with personnel hour rate schedules and budget estimates for completion of the project by International Asbestos Removal, Inc. At one point, the total projected cost for removal and decontamination of about 45,000 boxes of records from the State Records Center was 2.5 million dollars. The process of decontaminating the records and moving them from the State Record Center to Capital Records Management took over eight months. It was almost a year before the process was completed. The operation of the Public Records Administration was severely handicapped by not having an office and telephones after the fire forced the agency out of the State Records Center. Temporary office space in the Office of Veterans Affairs in the Veterans Memorial Building was given to the staff of the Public Records Administration, but it took weeks to get telephones installed in the area. Later, office space was found for the staff in the new Department of Administration Building when the building was completed before the end of the year.

Just before the fire, the National Historical Publications and Records Commission awarded a grant to the state in 1988 to establish a professional State Archives program. With the funding from this NHPRC grant, a complete survey of the archival records held by the State Records Center, the State Archives, and other state and local agencies was conducted by Inez Dillon Prinster, D.Ed., and Mark Conrad, who were hired as consultants under the grant project. The survey identified one-fourth to one-third of the records in the State Records Center as archival material. That survey helped greatly with the move of the records from the State Records Center. Mark Conrad developed a database for the records in dBase IV and helped to identify the records as they were moved. The grant resulted in the passage of *the State Archives and Historical Records Act* (*P.L. 1989, ch. 341; RIGL 42-8.1*), authored by Albin Wagner while he was still the Public Records Administrator, the creation of a Special Legislative Commission on the Archives, the procurement of a temporary site for the State Archives at 337 Westminster Street in downtown Providence, and the hiring of the first professionally trained State Archivist, Timothy A. Slavin.

In October 1989 Tim Slavin, previously a professional archivist for the Archdiocese of Chicago, was hired for the position of the State Archivist, as part of the new State Archives Program under the Secretary of State, Kathleen S. Connell, just in time for the 200th anniversary of statehood for Rhode Island, the last of the original thirteen states to join the Union in 1790. During those two hundred years, efforts to establish a State Archives ebbed and waned, producing only sporadic results. In 1893, an important survey entitled *The Town Records of Rhode Island* provided the first comprehensive information about the historical records of the state. The survey, researched and written by Amos Perry of the Rhode Island Historical Society, included nineteen questions ranging from the identification of separate record series (land evidence, town meeting proceedings, vital records, et cetera) to the type of office furnishings and records equipment. Such attention, however, was not always the common practice. The first State Records Commissioner was not established until 1896, while a legislative committee on records was not erected until 1944.

The first State Archivist, Phyllis Silva, worked alone in the Secretary of State's Office for twenty-one years as custodian of records of the General Assembly, Governor's Office, and other state agencies deposited there. Interest in family history mushroomed after Secretary of State August P. LaFrance appointed Silva, a former school teacher and active Democrat, to the position of overseeing the records of the General Assembly in 1968. Although not trained as an archivist, she grew into her job and became an expert in genealogy. By the time she retired in January 1989, the collection had grown to an office in the basement of the State House with an adjacent vault containing 970 cubic feet of records, including birth, deaths, and marriages, old land transactions, wills, divorces, and arrangements for orphaned children before 1853. With few exceptions, the Archives only held records of the state before the Civil War. More recent records were in the State Records Center, state offices, and collections scattered around the state. Although the Archives had some valuable records dating back to the 17th century, it had no environmental control or formal archival program for the collection, appraisal, description, and reference services for archival material.

In 1989 Albin Wagner resigned to take a faculty position with the master of archival studies (MAS) program in the School of Library, Archival and Information Studies at the University of British Columbia in Vancouver, British Columbia. Mark Conrad also left to become the Data Archivist at Pennsylvania State University. He later took a position in the Center for Electronic Records at the National Archives and Records Administration and is now the coordinator for the electronic records grants program of NHPRC.

The State Archives moved on June 1, 1990, to a renovated building at 337 Westminster Street in downtown Providence. The new home for the State Archives was dedicated by Secretary of State Kathleen S. Connell on October 26, 1990 with a gala ceremony, including an honor guard of historic militia units in the state. Finally, in 1991 the Secretary of State introduced a bill (91-S 654, An Act Relating to Public Records Administration) in the Legislature amending Title 38 of the *General Laws* to consolidate the state records management program with the State Archives. The act made the State Archivist the Public Records Administrator and combined the Public Records Administration with the State Archives, under the Secretary of State. The constitution of the Public Records Advisory Council, renamed the Public Records Advisory Commission, was changed and the Secretary of State replaced the Public Records Administrator as the chair of the body. David Maslyn, who recommended a consolidated program in the original "Maslyn Report," and others supported the consolidation of the archives and records management programs.

At the time of the fire in the State Records Center in 1989, it was estimated that about one-fourth to one-third of approximately 50,000 cubic feet of records in the Records Center were archival material. Today, most of those records have been moved from Capital Records Management to the State Archives under the present State Archivist, R. Gwenn Stearn, at 337 Westminster Street. Capital Records continues to serve as the State Records Center and to provide low-cost storage and retrieval services for the state records management program. The space formerly occupied in the Veterans Memorial Building by the State Record Center has been renovated to become, what it was intended to be by·its original builders: a large banquet hall.

What lessons were learned from the recovery from the fire in the State Records Center? You may be the judge of that. But there are several obvious ones. First of all, the experience demonstrated the importance of having a *Disaster Response Plan*. Rhode Island was fortunate that such a plan was being formulated when the fire took place, especially that the new commercial records center, Capital Records Management, was nearby with available storage space and that arrangements had been made to move records there in the event of a disaster. Information was also available about vendors and sources for disaster recovery supplies and equipment. Some disaster recovery supplies had been stored at the State Records Center Annex in the Matrix Building to aid in the recovery of records in case of a disaster in a state or local government agency. Contacts had been made for a facility in Providence to freeze-dry records, but the state was not able to use it in the case of the fire due to the fact that the records were contaminated with asbestos. It was a surprise to everyone that State Records Center was the first beneficiary of this planning.

What was not done was to make arrangements for a clear line of authority to make decisions and contract with vendors in case of a major disaster when key administrators are not available. Certainly, there was no previous arrangements to contract for asbestos abatement, purchase or rent equipment, or rent trucks. The operation of the Public Records Administration was severely handicapped by not having office space and telephones after the fire forced them out of the State Records Center. Most importantly, although the state was aware of the presence of asbestos in the Veterans Memorial Building, the problem was not addressed until just before the fire. A major renovation of the building was about to begin. Asbestos abatement projects can be very expensive, but asbestos abatement, just in the Veterans Memorial Building may have cost the state as much as $2.5 million. Removal of the asbestos would have been only a fraction of that cost if it had been done before the fire.

Some lessons were learned with the move from the State Records Center. First of all, the move emphasized the importance of good documentation of a collection and tight physical and intellectual control. We learned more about asbestos and asbestos abatement than we might ever care to know. Having trained personnel on site and part of the process was found to be essential to the success of the move. Training and certification of Public Records Administration staff members was found to be necessary in this situation. Renting motorized conveyor belts, air handling equipment, and refrigerator trucks helped. The process of air-drying damp documents on racks in the "Arizona Room" at Capital Records Management worked very well. Except for very wet documents, freeze-drying was not necessary. The experience confirmed the importance of a strong archival program and a secure, environmentally controlled archival storage facility. It showed very clearly an example of concrete results of the NHPRC grants and the contribution the grant program has made to the archives and records management programs all across the country, including Rhode Island. Most of all, the value of the dedicated staff of the Public Records Administration and Capital Records Management was demonstrated over and over again during the eight months to a year that it took to move the records.

Oregon Historical Society

Todd Welch

There comes a time in the history of every institution when circumstances force that institution to confront and accept new challenges. Moving a major research library's support facility should be considered paramount among those challenges. The Oregon Historical Society's (OHS) library staff and artifact collections management recently completed the demanding and exhaustive task of moving their collections from an old warehouse, built in 1922, in Northwest Portland to a new support facility in Gresham, Oregon. During the process the staff discovered a great deal more about their collections and themselves. This is the story of that great journey, its accomplishments and its challenges.

The Oregon Historical Society, established in 1898, operates as a private non-profit institution headquartered at the Oregon History Center in the cultural district of downtown Portland, Oregon. For more than six generations, the Society has served many different constituencies and built a great reputation as a community and cultural resource. Its primary responsibility is the recording and preservation of Oregon and Pacific Northwest heritage. The depth and breadth of primary resource materials maintained and available to the research public at the historical society have few rivals in the region. Library collections include books, newspapers, periodicals, government documents, film archives, manuscripts, maps, oral histories, and photographs. The sheer bulk of the collections and associated equipment requires that the institution store most of its resources at an off-site facility. This facility serves a vital role for the society. Besides storing library special collections and over 85,000 artifact items, it also acts as a reservoir for the unprocessed collections backlog and storage for the Oregon Historical Society Press, as well as the preliminary staging area for exhibits. It represents space and flexibility, two aspects valued by collection management staff.

Sale of Old Warehouse

In the early 1980s the historical society acquired a department store's old warehouse located in Northwest Portland's Pearl District. The four-story warehouse (only fifteen city blocks from the Oregon Historical Society's history center) allowed the institution to store and maintain its library materials, artifact collections, and exhibit furnishings near the center of the city's downtown metropolitan area. The location proved so valuable that the institution also leased the remaining vacant space on a monthly basis to Portland area libraries for housing their supplementary collections.

The old warehouse, dubbed the Beaver House in honor of the Hudson's Bay Company headquarters in London, held the overflow of manuscripts, architectural plans, institutional archives, government documents, periodicals, photographs and negatives, safety and nitrate film, maps, bound newspapers, newspaper clipping files, books, artifacts, Oregon Historical Society Press storage, and exhibit supplies that the historical society had collected and protected during its existence. These materials were stored in and on a variety of stationary shelving, filing cabinets, and pallets set on the warehouse floor. Some of the material was fully processed and cataloged, but a significant percentage of the collection was unprocessed and required reappraisal, deaccessioning or simple preservation work, and processing. While most of the material had specific shelf or pallet location designations, a fraction of material could not be readily identified or found. The library registrar and other staff spent countless patient hours trying to find materials or determine the contents of unidentified boxes.

The Beaver House also housed a carpentry workshop, nitrate film vault, film and video lab, photograph darkroom and studio, microfilming studio, and conservation lab. The historical society had ceased to do in-house microfilming or perform anything except the most basic conservation services during the last decade, but the dedicated space allowed the society the option to resurrect these services in the future.

The warehouse had its limitations. The building's engineering and environmental problems included an antiquated electrical system, a pre-World War Two boiler that was often temperamental and eventually broke down, windows that did not provide stable environmental conditions for long-range collection storage, and corroded water pipes. In spite of these shortcomings, the collection management staff adapted and grew to appreciate the vintage building. Throughout the 1990s the Beaver House proved convenient and functional for the historical society.

In August 2000, the historical society sold the warehouse facility. The buyers gave the historical society six months to find a new location and move its entire holdings into an as-yet-undetermined new facility.

Assembling the Move Team

The board and management formed a facilities committee to conduct a search of possible new locations in the Portland metropolitan area. It also was responsible for purchasing and, if necessary, renovating a new facility. The stated goal of the project was to find a structure that would provide improved environmental conditions for the society's materials. The chief operating officer assured the staff that the board recognized the historical society's primary responsibility to maintain and preserve the collections.

To find an appropriate location and protect the materials during the moving process, collection management staff stressed the need for improved internal communication and coordination between the collections and facilities staffs. In addition, the library program managers lobbied for accessibility to architects, engineers, vendors, contractors, and other consultants retained for the warehouse relocation. Daunting and tremendous as it may have appeared that early autumn day in 2000, the warehouse move gave the institution and its staff an opportunity to challenge old assumptions and forge a new era of cooperation.

The board and management also felt it was important to keep the library open during the relocation process and requested that the disruption to customer services and patron research be kept to a minimum. This resulted in two immediate measures. First, library staff and the historical society's information office launched a series of press releases and postings throughout the history center and via the society's mailings and web site. The message asked library patrons to remain patient during the ongoing warehouse relocation project and bear with the fact that some collections would be inaccessible during the process. Staff had to regularly explain to library patrons that the relocation project would improve the society's ability to preserve and protect research materials in the future. Even though the library reference staff instructed patrons that items at the warehouse were unavailable during the move and impending build-out, it was necessary to have the move team retrieve a few urgently needed materials before the move was complete.

Convinced that someone from outside the organization was needed to coordinate move-related activities for the library and alleviate some of the staff's greatly-increased work levels and stress, the chief operating officer, with the support of the library program managers, hired a two-person consulting team to provide leadership and facilitate most aspects of the library portion of the warehouse move. In hindsight, this decision proved crucial to the overall success of the endeavor. The consulting team possessed the ideal mixture of previous professional experience, organizational skills, and articulate tact to motivate and coordinate the library staff and collections management team during the warehouse relocation project. The consulting team deserves high praise for their efforts throughout the endeavor. The team's key responsibilities included: reviewing potential new warehouse locations to determine that they met the site and space planning criteria established by the society's management and curatorial staff; setting move-related goals and deadlines to ensure smooth coordination; organizing tasks and assigning specific responsibilities; and acting as conduits of communication and clarification among library staff, upper-level project managers, and outside agents. As a buffer between the library staff and other people involved with the move, they proved to be a highly effective team that accomplished an extraordinary amount in a short period of time while maintaining their professionalism and sense of humor.

The second measure that the historical society took to accommodate both library reference services and the move was to hire temporary staff to assist in the preparation and staging of the collections at both the old and new warehouse locations. The temporary workers included former work-study students and volunteers whose past experience at the historical society made the hiring process a relatively simple one. Job requirements included an appreciation for the integrity and significance of the historical society collections, an ability to work with a minimum of supervision, an aptitude to follow directions and perform work with attention to detail, and the willingness to work in less-than-ideal conditions. These workers performed collection preparation tasks throughout the relocation process. Working alongside the permanent staff and consulting team, the temporary workers were vital to the overall success of the project.

The historical society also secured the services of a professional moving company to execute the actual loading and transport of collections to the new support facility. The company specialized in library and special collection moves and proved itself reliable during an earlier reconfiguration of the historical society library's reading room. The importance of having an experienced, responsive moving company cannot be overstated. Moving company employees had an understanding of the fragility and uniqueness of the special collections materials, the security concerns among collection management staff, and the efficient and systematic process required to meet project deadlines. The outstanding performance of the professional movers allowed staff to concentrate on packing and staging materials rather than diverting attention and energy to transporting collections.

Collection Preparation and Packing

Beginning in October 2000, the consulting team, with the collaboration of library program managers, began identifying space coordination considerations, and assigning appropriate professional staff to answer questions and prepare library collections and equipment for the impending move. Questions of process, timelines, identified tasks, and overall project goals were addressed and explained to permanent and temporary employees in order to coordinate work and to provide staff with as much current and accurate information as possible. The project direction and objectives had to be clarified early so that the move team could successfully prepare and pack library collections for the physical move, scheduled to begin in the middle of January 2001. The effort to keep an open line of communication served to develop a relationship of trust and employee investment in the overall project.

An important aspect in the pre-move planning was the consulting team's analysis of the warehouse holdings and layout. The first priority was the protection of the collections. The consulting team determined the appropriate sequence of tasks, the expertise necessary to complete each task, and the optimal use of temporary help. A description of each pre-move task was recorded on a master list, along with a target deadline and the supervising staff member. Library move team meetings, held on a weekly basis, provided staff with the opportunity to report their progress. These meetings helped professional and project staff appreciate the incremental steps forward and promoted team unity. Parties were also scheduled on a regular basis to celebrate the project's progress and completion of benchmarks. Furthermore, the library move team was given special blue T-shirts and hot-pink name badges for identification and security purposes; these soon became a uniform that encouraged cooperation and teamwork.

The preparation and packing of collections and the dismantling of shelves occupied nearly three months of the project. The consulting team worked with key library personnel to estimate and order supplies for the protection and packing of collection materials. Materials included a variety of archival storage boxes, acid-free folders, linen tape, Velcro closures, bubble and shrink-wrap, labels, and wood pallets.

Procedures were instituted to track collections through the moving process. Permanent staff typically spent one to two days per week working alongside temporary staff to prepare the collections for the move. Tasks included replacing damaged boxes or handling unprocessed materials. The boxes were then palletized, including tagging and shrink-wrapping for tracking during the impending move. Alphanumeric and color-coded designations were developed for each collection category (that is, processed and unprocessed manuscripts: MSS001 or AMC001, maps: MAP001, photographs: PHO001, et cetera). This system improved tracking, and aided in statistically quantifying the materials ready to move. A computer database recorded each pallet ready for eventual transport to the new facility. Information included the collection name, number of boxes from the collection on the pallet, and any other details that may influence handling or moving. This database also proved useful in locating specific items when urgently needed.

Project staff were given additional training on how to package glass negatives, lantern slides, nitrate film, maps, and architectural and engineering drawings for the move. For example, staff rejacketed and reboxed many of the glass negatives, including inserting bubble wrap sheets at the front and back of each box to protect the negatives from shifting which otherwise could cause chipping or cracking. These boxes were boldly labeled, "Glass fragile" and carefully loaded on the upper shelf of the moving carts provided by the moving company; less fragile materials were packed on the lower shelf to stabilize the weight. The entire cart was shrink-wrapped to prevent any shifting of the boxes of glass. Dozens of carts were used so that they could be packed and wrapped ahead of the actual move.

Likewise, unprocessed maps and architectural drawings that had been rolled and stored in boxes during the accessioning process were either flattened into oversized map folders and placed in specially constructed pallet boxes or rehoused in custom-made telescoping rectangular archival boxes. These methods protected the oversized materials during the move.

The final materials to be moved were the nitrate film holdings, both moving picture and still photograph negatives. To meet the stringent code regulations for storage of nitrate materials,[1] the historical society chose to store the unstable medium off site until a safe, environmentally stable vault could be constructed at the support facility. A commercial film storage facility in Van Nuys, California, was selected based on their experience and reliability.

The film archivist, following HazMat Classification 4.1 regulations, supervised the handling and packaging of the nitrate motion picture film into regulation size cardboard boxes labeled "flammable solid." These boxes were then fitted into larger cardboard boxes with the same specified labeling. A few films were found to be in deteriorating condition. These were isolated and disposed of through a local hazmat disposal service. The process of boxing the nitrate motion picture film took nearly three weeks.

Other professional staff worked on the packing of still photograph nitrate negatives and reels of negatives for aerial photographs. These nitrate materials were packed in archival boxes and wrapped in polyethylene bags before being placed in prescribed cardboard boxes labeled with "flammable solids" stickers. To prevent the archival document boxes from sliding around inside the outer box, any gaps were filled with vermiculite placed in zip-lock plastic bags to ensure that the combustible items remained as stable as possible during the move. The plastic bags controlled the dust created by the vermiculite.

A trucking company licensed to move flammable materials had been selected by the consultants to transport the materials to Southern California. There the nitrate collections were stored in an environmentally controlled vault until the construction of approved storage vaults had been completed at the support facility in Gresham.

The last area to be disassembled and staged for the move was the video lab. The specialized knowledge necessary to accomplish this task without damaging the fragile and valuable equipment required contracting with an outside engineer. The engineer worked with the film archivist to pack the equipment and move it to the new support facility after the completion of the library move.

The New Warehouse

Beginning in late September 2000, the facilities committee retained a real estate brokerage firm to explore locations for a new support facility. The collections and facilities staff drafted a support facility space needs analysis worksheet. The worksheet itemized the activities required or desired at the future support facility, and the space requirements for museum and library storage, as well as the square footage needed for support areas and common spaces. These documents gave the realtors a blueprint to evaluate available property in the Portland metropolitan area. The facilities committee visited multiple sites and recommended to the board the purchase of a warehouse in Gresham (located thirteen miles east of the Oregon History Center).

The new support facility contains nearly 120,000 square feet of space. Architects and engineers were hired to design floor plans that accounted for the following spaces: library and artifact storage areas; collections receiving; dirty processing and clean processing rooms;

moving-image office and video lab; nitrate film vaults with separate environmental monitoring and controls; conservation lab; exhibits fabrication and storage areas; security station; public research room; staff meeting room; and adequate restrooms. Library staff suggested the most efficient layout of collection storage and shared work areas. The initial visions of the support facility were later altered to meet budgetary and staffing realities. Library staff stressed the importance of separate staging areas for dirty and clean processing to stage and work on recent accessions. These spaces survived further alterations to the floor plan; however, the conservation lab became an early casualty during the planning process, although space was allowed for future development.

Meanwhile, plans for a major renovation of the new support facility were put on hold until after the completion of the collections move. Renovation plans included a new roof, plumbing and electrical enhancements, additional insulation, specialized storage and processing areas, and improved heating, venting, and air-conditioning equipment to stabilize the environmental conditions for specific storage areas inside the building.

The Move Begins

Starting January 10, 2001, the moving company began transporting collection materials from the Beaver House to the new Gresham Support Facility. The project move team was subdivided into the "origin" party and the "destination" party. Each member of the respective parties was responsible for an aspect of the moving process: identifying and tracking the pallets or carts loaded or unloaded at each site, staging materials into predefined areas at the new site, and reporting any problems or concerns to the move consultant team and the professional moving company representative. The consultant team's planning and the project staff's preparation were rewarded. It took the moving company twenty one days to load seventy two truckloads of library collections, transport them between the two facilities, and unload them into the Gresham Support Facility.

The consulting team developed a floor plan so that members of the destination party could instruct or assist movers in staging the collections onto pallet shelving or newly installed Spacesaver shelving. The Spacesaver shelving was a donation from local commercial banks that had used the mobile shelving units in their record centers. The unloading and reshelving process took time, but the importance of maintaining physical and intellectual control of the collections was vital to future collection accessibility. Unfortunately, some collections, such as the maps and architectural drawings, had to be left on pallets until the new facility construction had been completed and additional shelving assembled.

By February 14, 2001, 98 percent of the collections had been moved. The remaining research materials, furnishings, and equipment were packed and staged for transport to the Gresham Support Facility. Based on approximately twenty weeks of preparation and moving, the number of estimated hours dedicated to the library move totaled nearly 5,900. Everyone associated with the move—the board, management, staff, and the movers themselves—was impressed and relieved at the success of the enterprise.

The Build-Out

The collection preparation and move phases of the relocation project were quite successful; however, the build-out work at the new support facility, while essential for the long-term care and preservation of the library materials, exposed the collections to undesirable environmental conditions. Due to the time pressures imposed on the historical society by the sale of the Beaver House and the move to Gresham, the board and management were not able to purchase and renovate a new support facility before moving the collections. The urgency to find a new facility and move dictated a short timeline.

Now that the collections had been packed, moved, and most of the materials reshelved, the construction and renovation could begin at the new support facility. In early spring project staff began covering shelving units with a thick plastic barrier to protect them from dust and other by-products of construction that could harm them. It was also necessary to have members of the library staff continuously present to observe the construction work and report any concerns or problems related to the preservation or security of the collections to the society's facilities staff and the on-site construction manager. The library registrar and his assistants coped with the following conditions during the build-out: planned power outages; lack of computer and phone access; jackhammer and demolition noises; and constant fluctuations of temperature and relative humidity in the collection storage areas. These were not ideal conditions for staff or collections, but temporary inconveniences necessary to create a highly functional support center.

The contractors and facilities staff worked on the following projects: pulling down interior walls and framing new storage and work spaces; removing the majority of the drafty exterior loading-dock doors; tearing up concrete floors to install new water pipes; replacing and upgrading the electrical system and environmental controls; installing new security, fire-suppression, and telecommunications systems; installing additional wall insulation and a new roof; and painting outside and inside the building. Throughout the build-out process, the library registrar and collection management staff had to coordinate activities with facilities staff and, often, served as an advocate for the welfare of the collections.

One of the most challenging components of the build-out was the design and construction of nitrate vaults with separate environmental controls that allow staff to set and monitor conditions. The film archivist and other library staff consulted the professional literature and experts in the field, and advised the engineers on a plan that would meet Gresham's fire and building code regulations. These plans needed to be filed with the city buildings bureau and a permit obtained before construction could begin. Likewise, the completed vaults including shelving configuration had to be examined by inspectors before a use permit could be issued.

Major construction at the facility ended in August, and library staff returned to complete shelving of the photo and film collections in the enclosed, climate-controlled area reserved for them. In early September 2001, the library staff closed the reference room for a week and worked at the new support facility. The primary objective during the closure was to assemble more shelving and align it according to the specifications on the floor plan.

The inspection process necessary to acquire a permit of occupancy is quite extensive. Fire and building inspectors visited the new facility on multiple occasions to list the modifications needed to comply fully with established codes and regulations. Wiring and electrical outlets, proper wall and floor anchoring of shelving, aisle spacing, and egress lighting needed to pass code before permits could be issued. By December 2001, it began to appear that the long relocation project had come to a close. This fifteen-month journey tested the library and facilities staffs, but the resulting support facility made special collections colleagues in the region envious.

Accomplishments

The new support facility will serve the Oregon Historical Society well into the future. It is an incredible accomplishment, and the board, management, and staff were satisfied with the overall outcome, but many other tangible benefits also resulted from the collection move. These included the opportunity to reappraise and deaccession materials that did not meet the historical society's collection policy, the opportunity to offer surplus equipment and shelving to affiliate historical museums, and the chance to organize and conduct a closed auction of the society's out-of-field sale and trade items to benefit the library acquisition and preservation fund.

For years the collections management staff speculated that, if given the time and staffing, many collections could be reappraised for deaccession and donated to more appropriate institutions. Before and particularly during the relocation project, staff identified specific opportunities. Examples include the transfer of thousands of out-of-field glass lantern slides to the Magic Lantern Castle Museum in San Antonio, Texas; the donation of Slavic and Southeast Asian periodicals and journals to the University of Washington and Portland State University; the relocation of selected papers to Willamette University in Salem, Oregon; and the return of deed books to the Multnomah County Archives Program. Even though the staff did not reappraise as much as they had hoped to during the project, the evaluation led to great advances in removing out-of-field items from the holdings and reducing library storage space. It also gave the historical society an opportunity to build goodwill and to network with other cultural and educational institutions.

Early in the project it became apparent that the society's surplus furniture and equipment stored at the Beaver House could prove useful to the county and city museum members belonging to the Oregon Historical Society's Affiliates Program.[2] The society's field service coordinator invited representatives from the affiliate organizations to visit the old warehouse to select surplus items. Deaccessioned furniture included shelving, wooden flat file units, tables, desks, chairs, and wooden file cabinets. This process allowed the historical society to network and assist the affiliates in their own endeavors.

The accumulation of out-of-field trade and sale books, periodicals, and government documents over the years was quite sizable. Little had been done during the previous decade to reduce the number of items and the storage space they required, but the move presented an opportunity for library staff to dispose of these materials and benefit the remaining collections at the same time. The consulting team suggested that the library conduct a closed auction among regional book dealers for components of the trade and sale items. Invitations were sent to dealers who scheduled appointments to view the offerings and make bids. By December 2000, the auction was closed and those with the winning bids were notified. The profits from the auction were deposited into the library acquisition and preservation fund to be used to purchase new library materials and pay for collection maintenance and repair.

Summary

Of course the accomplishment that will have the most lasting impact on the Oregon Historical Society is the acquisition of a new support facility. The new building is the pride and joy of the collections and facilities staffs. It is cleaner and more environmentally stable than the Beaver House. It also represents improvements in storage space, lighting, and shared work areas. The move allowed library staff to gain greater physical and intellectual control over the collections and provides for larger, dedicated spaces for processing and reference services. The relocation project did exactly what the board had requested. It provided the collections with a superior support facility. Let us hope that we do not have to move for another twenty years!

Acknowledgments

The author would like to recognize the invaluable leadership of Glenn and Judith Mason for their role in the move, as well as the hard work and dedication shown by library registrar Matt Oftedahl during the entire relocation project. The library move team consisted of the following members: Andrew Bryans, Daniel Davidson, Richard Engeman, Steve Hallberg, Sharon Howe, Bob Kingston, Peter Kopp, Michele Kribs, Rich Read, Susan Seyl, Amanda Tillstrom, Mikki Tint, Johnyne Wascavage, Todd Welch, Elizabeth Winroth, and Larisa Zimmerman. This chapter could not have been possible without the wisdom of Susan Seyl and the editorial skills, advice, and good judgment of Sharon Howe and Mikki Tint.

Notes

1. A Nitrate film vault should be an isolated, purpose built depot exclusively used for the storage of nitrate material. The vaults should be partitioned into fire resistant, concrete compartments, each of which should hold a maximum of 2,500 Kg (approximately 300,000m or 1,000,000ft) of nitrate film. The vaults should be as small as possible.

Each vault should have doors opening outwards onto a corridor and be equipped with pressure vents to the outside.   The depot should be fully air-conditioned and the temperature and relative humidity should be continuously measured, recorded, and monitored.   Fire alarm and extinguishing systems should be as sophisticated as can be afforded.   In the event of a fire, only local sprinklers, in the burning vault or vaults should be activated to cool the walls to prevent the fire from spreading. Water in vaults that are not burning would damage the remaining nitrate collection.   The alarm system should warn not only of the outbreak of fire but of the malfunction of the air conditioning and of unauthorized entry to the storage areas.   For more information on nitrate film storage standards, see *Audiovisual Archives: A Practical Reader.* UNESCO, 1997.

2. In 1945 The Oregon Historical Society formally established a strong cooperative network with a small number of county historical societies in Oregon.   Since that time OHS has developed its Affiliate program to include over 138 diverse historical organizations working actively throughout the state.   This mutually beneficial program is designed to promote the exchange of information and professional expertise between, and among, OHS and its affiliated county and local historical agencies and organizations.

About the Contributors

Lisa Backman, head librarian at the Barco Library, The Cable Center in Denver, Colorado, is responsible for library and archives activities such as reference and research questions, editing the website and the processing of archives. Prior to The Cable Center, she was the manuscript specialist in the Western History and Genealogy Department at the Denver Public library where she worked for fifteen years. She also served as a research librarian at the Boston Athenaeum. She holds a Master of Arts degree in American history with a certificate in Historical Agencies and Administration from Northeastern University, a Master of Science degree in library science from Simmons College and a Bachelor of Arts degree in American history from Framingham State College in Massachusetts. She is past president, vice president and secretary of the Society of Rocky Mountain Archivists. For the past three years she has taught collection development and appraisal at the Library and Archives Institute in Massachusetts.

Gary Harrington is a certified archivist who has held a variety of archival and research management positions at Oklahoma Department of Libraries since 1979. Currently he is the Administrative Archivist within the library's Office of Government Information. In 1971 he earned a Bachelor of Arts degree in history at the College of the Ozarks in Clarksville, Arkansas and then received a Master of Arts degree in history from the State University of New York in Plattsburgh, New York in 1978. Prior to his employment with the Oklahoma Department of Libraries, he served seven and one-half years in the United States Air Force. He is a member of the Society of Southwest Archivists, the Oklahoma Conservation Congress, and the Academy of Certified Archivists. He has published an in-house article titled "The Oklahoma-Texas Boundary Dispute" which is an inventory of primary source materials concerning the Oklahoma-Texas boundary and United States Supreme Court decisions since 1923.

Walter Jones serves as the Assistant Head of the J. Willard Marriott Library's Special Collections Department at the University of Utah. In this position he supervises the department's Manuscripts Division and works with both the University of Utah's Archives and Records Manager and the Curator for Multi-media Archives. During the fall of 1998, he became the coordinator for Special Collections' move into permanent quarters in the Marriott Library and worked for the next ten months to assist in the planning and implementation of that move. In addition to having a Master's degree in library and information science, he holds a Master of Arts degree in history from the University of Utah and has written and published extensively about various topics relating to the history of the Rocky Mountain West. Two of his better-known works are *History of the Sand Bar, 1888-1977* (Casper, Wyoming: BASO, Inc., 1981) which is a history of Casper, Wyoming's red light district and an article titled "Petroleum" published in Allan Kent Powell's *Utah History Encyclopedia* (Salt Lake City, Utah: University of Utah Press, 1994).

Monte Kniffen currently works as the Archivist and Records Manager for the Denver Province of the Redemptorists in Denver, Colorado where he has been since 2001. He spent the previous four years working as an archivist at the American Heritage Center at the University of Wyoming. After receiving a Bachelor of Arts degree in history and sociology from Black Hills State University, he took his archival training from Colorado State University and graduated in 1997, earning a Master of Arts degree in public history with a concentration in archival science and records management. Having become a certified archivist while at the University of Wyoming, he is now a member of the Academy of Certified Archivists, the Society of American Archivists, the Society of Rocky Mountain Archivists, and the Colorado Preservation Alliance.

Joanne A. Mattern has been with the Delaware Public Archives for twenty-nine years as a curator, archivist, Deputy State Archivist, and Manager of Records Services. She is responsible for the planning and implementation of all activities that relate to the servicing, care and handling of records during all phases of the Delaware Public Archives new building construction, which began in 1995. Currently, she is involved in the final return of the records from storage and placing them in their home in the new facility. Joanne has long been a participant in regional and national professional organizations and workshops, has served on program committees, arrangement committees and as a speaker. She has also worked with the National Historical Publications and Records Commission on grants review committees and as a project consultant. Her publications include two works that she wrote jointly with Harold B. Hancock: "Special Collections in the Delaware State Archives: Small Manuscripts and Account Books," *Delaware History Magazine* 19, no. 3, (Spring-Summer 1981) and *A Preliminary Inventory of the Older Records in the Delaware Archives* (Dover, Delaware: Bureau of Archives and Records, 1978).

John Newman is Professor and University Archivist at Colorado State University. His undergraduate degree and Master of Library Science degree are from the University of Washington and his Master of Arts degree in history is from Colorado State University. He is a member of both the Academy of Certified Archivists and the Institute of Certified Records Managers. He lectures and writes extensively on professional and specialized topics. His *Vietnam War Literature* (third edition, Scarecrow Press, 1996) is the standard reference in the field. He has served as an officer of the Society of Rocky Mountain Archivists, the Colorado Library Association, and the Northern Colorado Chapter of Records Managers and Administrators. As a consultant, he specializes in the organization and documentation of large collections and moving archives.

Patrick M. Quinn holds the position of University Archivist at Northwestern University. He has been an archivist for thirty-six years, serving previously at the State Historical Society of Wisconsin and as Assistant University Archivist at the University of Wisconsin. He did his undergraduate and graduate work in English and history at the University of Wisconsin and holds a Certificate in Archival Administration from the American University. He teaches archival administration at Dominican University's Graduate School of Library and Information Science and in the Graduate History Program at Loyola University in Chicago, Illinois. He has contributed over three dozen articles and reviews to archival and historical publications, and is active in professional archival organizations. In addition he is a Fellow of the Society of American Archivists.

Russell C. Taylor is the head of reference services at Brigham Young University's L. Tom Perry Special Collections Department within the Harold B. Lee Library. Before becoming the head of reference at the Harold B. Lee Library, he worked as a reference librarian at Mary Washington College in Fredericksburg, Virginia, and at Anoka-Ramsey Community College in Coon Rapids, Minnesota. In addition he spent a number of years as a speech writer, a consultant, and as an employee of such organizations as the Federal Bureau of Investigation, the American Medical Association, Merck and Company, and Meditronic, Inc. He holds a Bachelor of Arts degree in history and a Masters of Library and Information Science degree from Brigham Young University, and later earned a Juris Doctor degree from Sycracuse University Law School.

Cassandra M. Volpe has served since 1999 as the archivist for the American Music Research Center and Glenn Miller Archive at the University of Colorado at Boulder, Music Library. She was the archivist for the Western Historical Collections and University of Colorado Archives from 1969 to 1998, serving as Acting Department Head and Curator from 1988 to 1990. Her areas of specialization are donor relations, visual resources, and music resources. She is a graduate of the University of Colorado at Boulder, National Archives' Modern Archives Institute, Wayne State University Introduction to Archives, Museums and Library Conservation, University of Denver Institute of Archival and Manuscript Management, and the Campbell Center for Historic Preservation Studies in Care of Photographic Collections. She has published several articles, the most recent being "Labor Collections in the Western Historical Collections at the University of Colorado, Boulder," reprinted in *Labor History Archives in the United States: A Guide for Research and Teaching*, edited by Daniel Leab and Philip P. Mason (Detroit, Michigan: Wayne State University Press, 1992), and "Brief Collection Descriptions of the American Music Research Center Archives," *American Music Research Center Journal*, 10 (2000).

Albin Wagner, formerly Public Records Administrator of the Rhode Island State Archives and Public Records Administration, is Chief of the Bureau of Records Management for the State of New Jersey and, as a Certified Records Manager and Certified Archivist, heads the New Jersey Division of Archives and Records Management's new initiative to create an electronic records program for state and local agencies. He holds Master's degrees in history from the University of Colorado and Harvard University and has earned a Certificate in Archives and Records Management from the Institute for Advanced Archival Studies at the University of Denver. He is the Manager of the Education Sector of the Industry Specific Group's program of the Association of Records Mangers and Administrators International. He has authored numerous articles and publications.

Todd Welch has, over the past seven years, worked in the manuscripts department of the Oregon Historical Society. His previous professional experience includes positions at the Oregon State Archives, Washington State Historical Society, and the Center for Pacific Northwest Studies at Western Washington University. He received his Bachelor of Science degree in history and sociology from Portland State University and his Master of Arts degree in history and archival administration from Western Washington University. He has published articles on environmental research in archives and manuscript repositories in the *American Archivists* and *Easy Access*, and has presented papers on many topics at several professional conferences. He is a member of the Society of American Archivists and an officer of Northwest Archivists.